texts 2 teens

Sending the advice and wisdom that they desperately need

Dr. Roger D. Smith

Author of *Advice written on the back of a business card*
and *Fortune Cookies: Small secrets on how to make a fortune*

Modelbenders Press

Texts 2 Teens: Sending the advice and wisdom that they desperately need.

Copyright 2010 by Roger Smith. All rights reserved. No part of this book may be reproduced or transmitted in any form or by any means, electronic or mechanical, including photocopying, recording, or by any information storage and retrieval system, without written permission from the author. For information address Modelbenders Press, P.O. Box 781692, Orlando, Florida 32878.

Modelbenders Press books may be purchased for business and promotional use or for special sales. For information please contact the publisher.

Visit our web site at www.modelbenders.com

PRINTED IN THE UNITED STATES OF AMERICA

Designed by Adina Cucicov at Flamingo Designs

The Library of Congress has cataloged the paperback edition as follows:

Smith, Roger
    Texts 2 Teens: Sending the advice and wisdom that they desperately need.
    Roger Smith – 1st ed.
    1. Family & Relationships: Life Stages—Teenager
    2. Business & Economics: Careers—General
    3. Self-Help: Personal Growth—Success
    I. Roger Smith   II. Title

ISBN-13: 978-0-9823040-8-2
ISBN-10: 0-9823040-8-0

Table of Contents

Text Messaging 3

Chapter 1: Actions 5

Chapter 2: Attitude 43

Chapter 3: Character 67

Chapter 4: Confidence 85

Chapter 5: Education 95

Chapter 6: Joy 121

Chapter 7: Love 129

Chapter 8: Relationships 137

Chapter 9: Work 155

Text Messaging

The first text message was sent from Neil Papworth to Richard Jarvis in December 1992. Neil used his computer and the Vodaphone network to send Richard the message "Merry Christmas". They started a small snowball of change rolling down a very long hill of electronic communication. It took nearly eight years to become a big success. By 2000, mobile phone owners were sending 17 billion messages per year. In 2001 it was up to 250 billion. By 2004 it was at 500 billion—or nearly 100 messages for every person on the planet.

With so many messages being typed, sent, and read, it is no wonder that your children do not have time to listen to all of the information that you and other adults have to share with them. They are being bombarded with an ocean of *"what up?"* and responding with *"nuthin you?"*

With all of these empty digits flying around the planet, there must be a way to inject some real wisdom and knowledge into the stream. There is certainly enough network capacity to carry as much knowledge and wisdom as you are willing to send.

Texting Wisdom

This book contains over 150 short words of wisdom and advice that you really wish you could get your kids to listen to. But since they won't listen when you talk, maybe you can catch them off

TEXTS 2 TEENS

Sending the advice and wisdom that they desperately need

guard with a text message. Maybe they will accidently pay a little attention to what you have to say if you inject it into the stream of messages that go directly to their brains.

The messages in this book were distilled from world leaders, successful professionals, and experienced parents. They are a good set go get started communicating with your distracted teenagers. Who knows, they may even pass them on to their friends. That would be an epidemic of good ideas in the global data stream. You could be responsible to spreading little seeds of wisdom and good character to dozens, hundreds, or thousands of young minds.

Once you get started with the ideas here, begin to create your own and just keep sending them. If the cell phone networks can carry billions of *"what up?"* messages every year, they can afford to carry a few really helpful words of wisdom along side of them.

In the United States, mobile phone owners average 188 text messages per month. Any teenager who is reading 47 text messages every week needs at least one with a little sage advice from you.

So start reading and start texting these ideas to the teenagers that you love.

Chapter 1

ACTIONS

TEXTS 2 TEENS

Sending the advice and wisdom that they desperately need

Ghandi
Indian Political Leader

Ghandi saw the injustice in India and made himself the change agent for the problem. He believed in personal responsibility and personal action to make the world a better place.

TEXTS 2 TEENS

Chapter 1: Actions

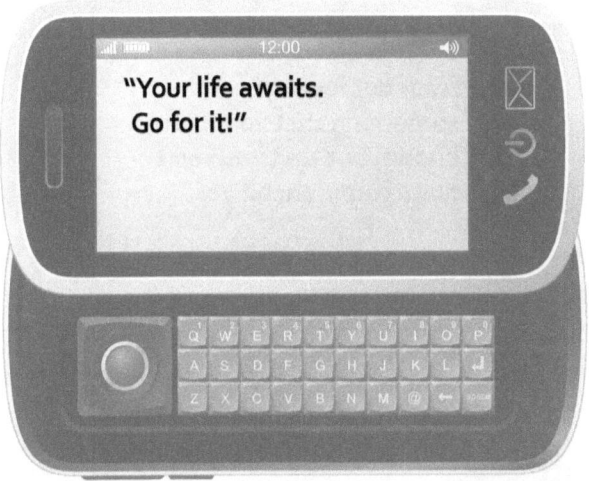

Phyllis Reardon
Life Coach

 Go find out what kind of wonderful things you can do in the world. It is going to be different from what anyone else has done.

TEXTS 2 TEENS

Sending the advice and wisdom that they desperately need

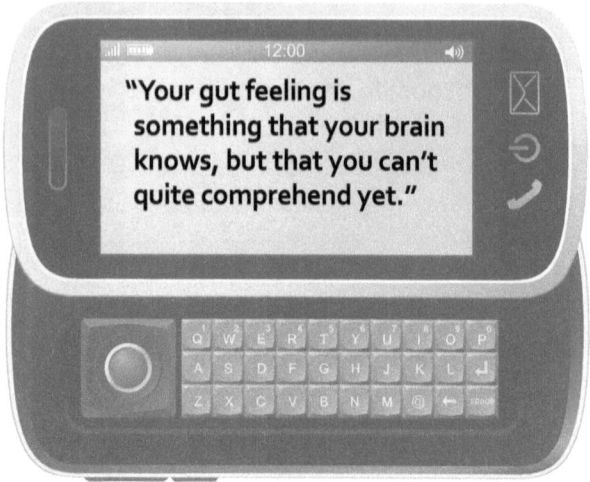

Fred Brumwell
Consultant

 Go with your gut. It is telling you something deeper than you consciously understand right now.

Chapter 1: Actions

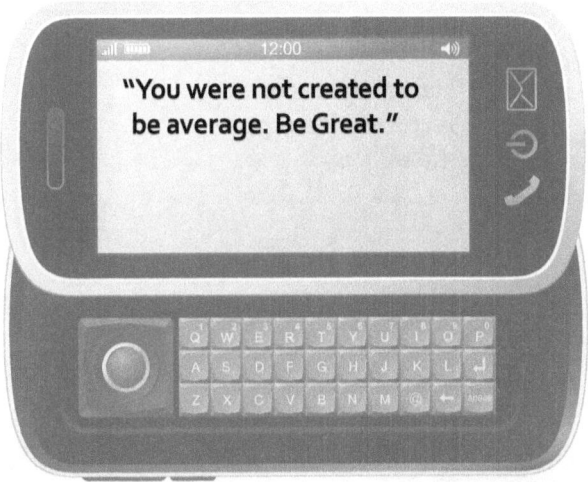

Benjamin Mena
Recruiter, Lockheed Martin

Who should be average in this world? The world is so big that there is room for everyone to be great at something.

TEXTS 2 TEENS

Sending the advice and wisdom that they desperately need

Woody Allen
Actor & Director

Most people are very lax in their work and their attendance. They miss days. They show up late. They leave early. You can be more successful than half of the world just by showing up consistently. Just by being there to do something.

TEXTS 2 TEENS

Chapter 1: Actions

 You cannot spend your life doing just the job that others want. You have to use your life to pursue your own interests and dreams.

TEXTS 2 TEENS

Sending the advice and wisdom that they desperately need

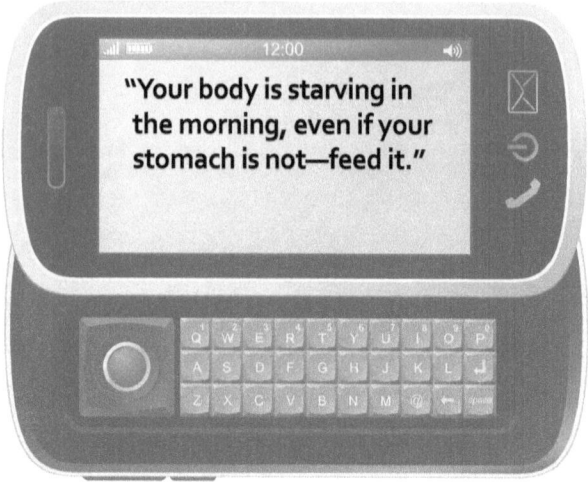

When you wake up you have just spent half of the day not eating. If you did that during the day you would know you were hungry. But because it happened while you slept, your body has not noticed how hungry it is yet.

TEXTS 2 TEENS

Chapter 1: Actions

 Successful cities have pushed nature's beauty out to the edges. Make a practice of going out to that edge to touch the beauty.

TEXTS 2 TEENS

Sending the advice and wisdom that they desperately need

Yoda
Jedi Master

 "Doing" leads to succeeding. "Trying" means you have decided to fail right from the start.

TEXTS 2 TEENS

Chapter 1: Actions

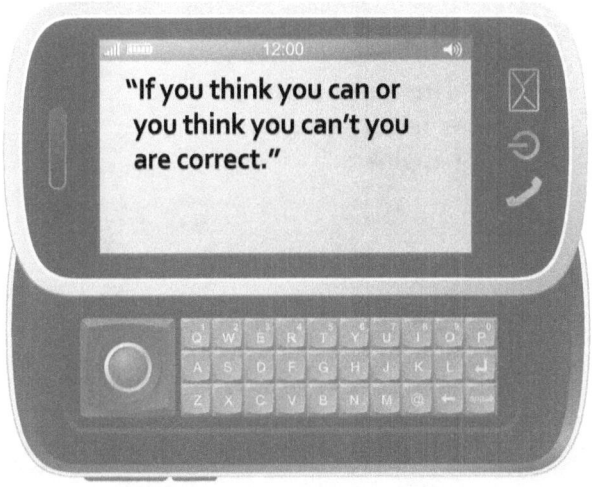

 All sports coaches know this and work on training their players attitudes just as much as they train their bodies.

TEXTS 2 TEENS

Sending the advice and wisdom that they desperately need

The ways to health, happiness, beauty, and peace are all well known and widely shared. But they are seldom followed because they are difficult. Stop looking for a secret and easy path, there isn't one.

TEXTS 2 TEENS

Chapter 1: Actions

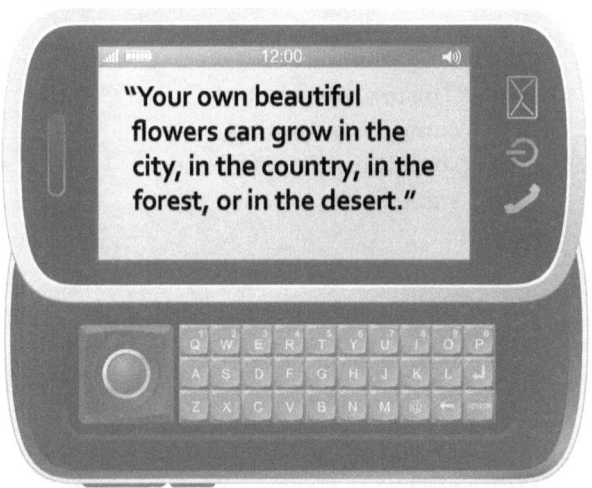

 You can bloom anywhere if you just choose to do so. Do not let a harsh environment stop you from growing and being a thing of beauty to all around you.

TEXTS 2 TEENS

Sending the advice and wisdom that they desperately need

 Humans were made to create and contribute to the world. One of the most rewarding things you can do is to add to or improve the world around you.

TEXTS 2 TEENS

Chapter 1: Actions

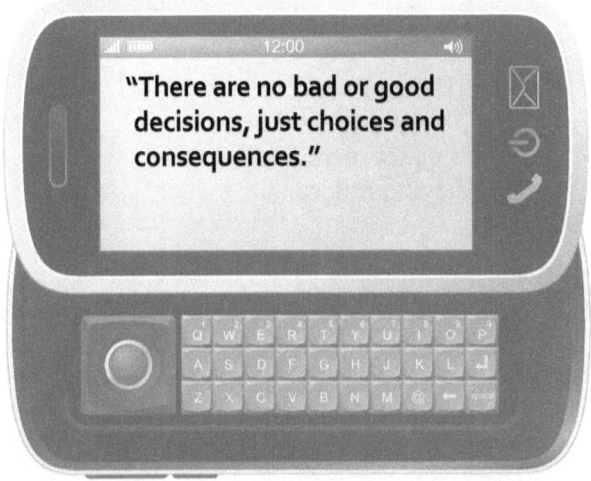

David Schwartz
Rochester Institute of Technology

When you make a choice to do something or not to do something, you are connected directly to the consequences of that action. What happens to you is usually not an accident, it is a consequence of your own actions.

TEXTS 2 TEENS

Sending the advice and wisdom that they desperately need

Dr. Dave Pratt
Chief Scientist, SAIC

 Don't do either of these until you are willing to live with the results for the rest of your life.

TEXTS 2 TEENS

Chapter 1: Actions

Ben Sawyer
Digital Mill

All parents are worried that you will drive, text, and crash. Phones were not created to make you a better driver, but they certainly do make you a worse one.

TEXTS 2 TEENS

Sending the advice and wisdom that they desperately need

Kevin Wilshere
President, The Analysis Group

The text message will still be there when you get to your destination. Let it wait.

TEXTS 2 TEENS

Chapter 1: Actions

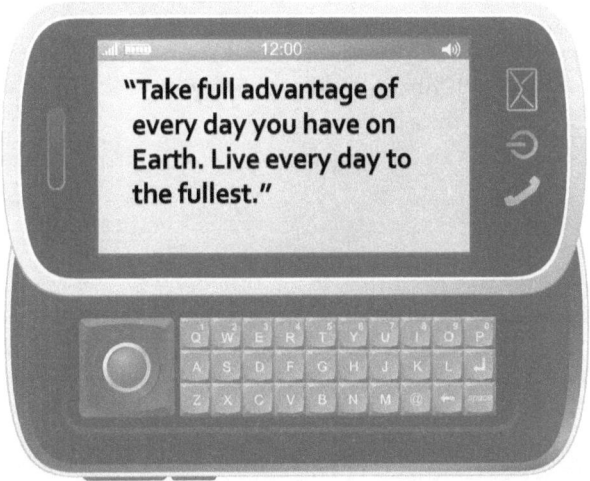

Eric Root
VP Engineering, Modus Operendi

There is something valuable and good to be done every day. You get better at seeing these opportunities as you get older. Seize these moments to make a difference.

TEXTS 2 TEENS

Sending the advice and wisdom that they desperately need

 You can live anywhere you want in the world. Look around and find a place that you really like.

Chapter 1: Actions

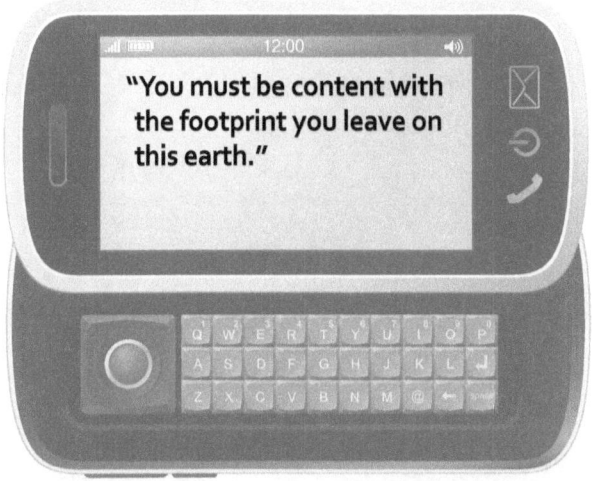

Bob Mcintosh
*Workshop Specialist,
Career Center of Lowell*

 We all leave thousands of footprints behind us as we life on the earth. Are you happy with the prints you have left and their impact on other people?

TEXTS 2 TEENS

Sending the advice and wisdom that they desperately need

"The harder you work, the luckier you get."

Rob Coble
*Career Development,
Full Sail University*

Luck does not fall magically from the sky. It is something that you earn by working at it.

TEXTS 2 TEENS

Chapter 1: Actions

Rod Olson
*Business Development Manager,
Rockwell Collins*

 Do not blame the world for the people and events around you. You are attracting them by your own actions.

TEXTS 2 TEENS

Sending the advice and wisdom that they desperately need

Mike Kalaf
Senior Manager, Lockheed Martin

 A well nourished, well rested person can take on any challenge.

TEXTS 2 TEENS

Chapter 1: Actions

Jeff Covelli
Program Manager, Northrop Grumman

 Life can be full of challenges, excitement, and fulfillment. Grab hold of it and get your share.

TEXTS 2 TEENS

Sending the advice and wisdom that they desperately need

 You can sleep as much as you want when you are dead. Take advantage of every moment while you are still alive.

TEXTS 2 TEENS

Chapter 1: Actions

Lisa Galarneau
User Experience Researcher, Microsoft

There are always new and interesting ideas in the world. Capture them before they flit away and you forget them.

TEXTS 2 TEENS

Sending the advice and wisdom that they desperately need

Rick Severinghaus
AEgis Technologies Group

You get to pick your lottery number and the winning number. You can't lose unless you decide to make yourself a loser.

TEXTS 2 TEENS

Chapter 1: Actions

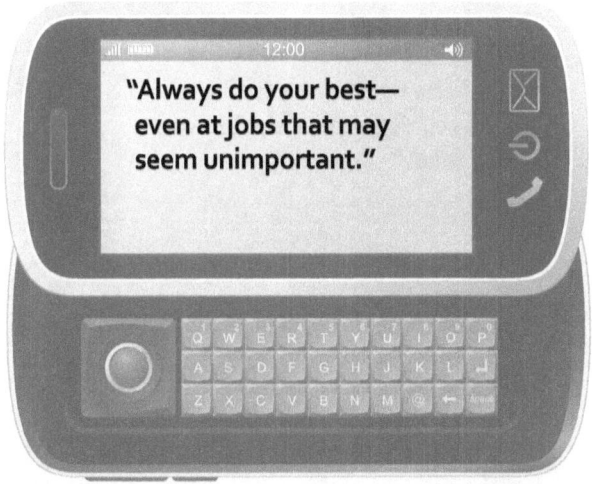

Dr. Doug Reece
Principle Scientist, ARA

The job that is not important to you is important to someone else. Do good work so you can enjoy the rewards that come from those who needed the work done.

TEXTS 2 TEENS

Sending the advice and wisdom that they desperately need

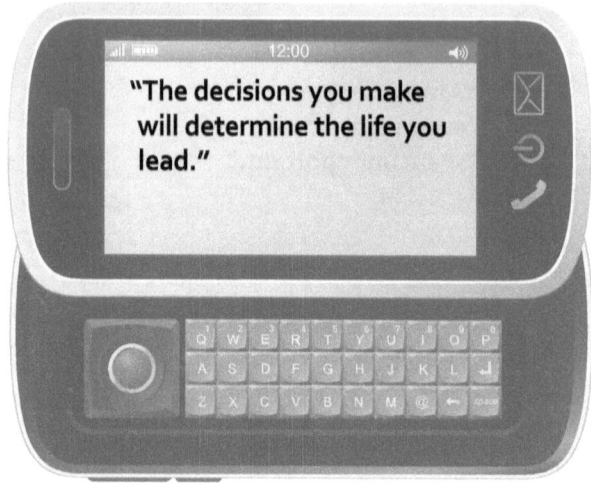

Mark Cawthorn
Captain, US Coast Guard

 Your life is the accumulated results of the decisions you have made. You are where you are because of what you have decided to do up to this point.

TEXTS 2 TEENS

Chapter 1: Actions

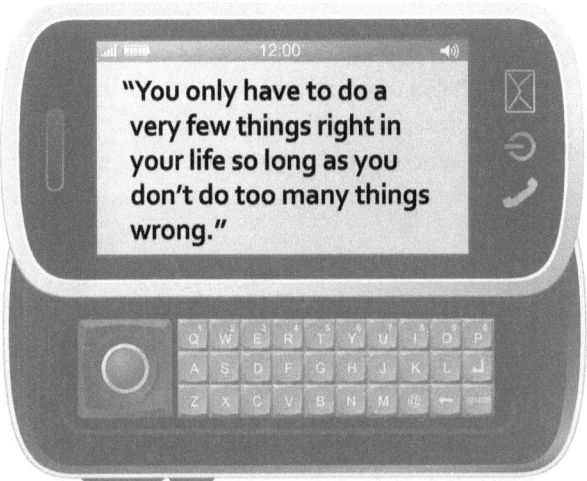

Warren Buffett
Investor

The rewards for doing a few things very well can support you for your whole life. Buffett has become the richest man in the world based on just a few skills that pay very well.

TEXTS 2 TEENS

Sending the advice and wisdom that they desperately need

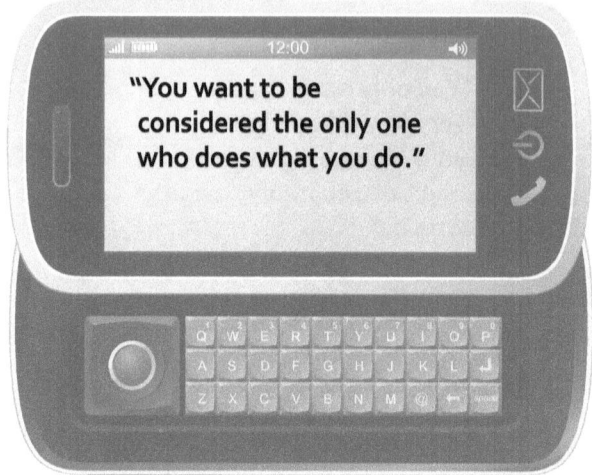

Jerry Garcia
Musician

Do not try to be the best at what everyone else is already doing. Find a path that is completely unique to you and add something original to the world.

TEXTS 2 TEENS

Chapter 1: Actions

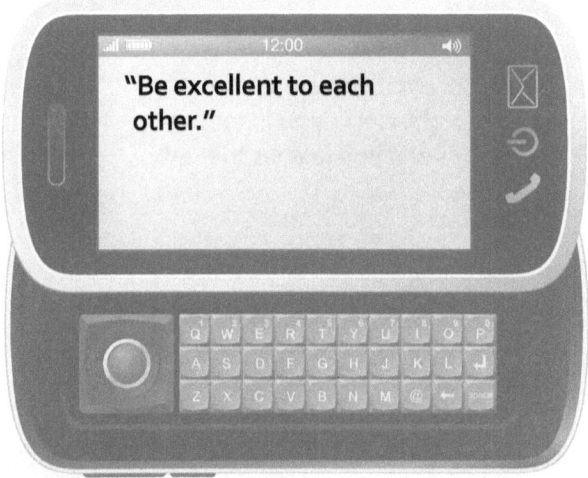

Bill & Ted's Excellent Adventure

 Bill and Ted were wise in the ways of treating other people... dude.

TEXTS 2 TEENS

Sending the advice and wisdom that they desperately need

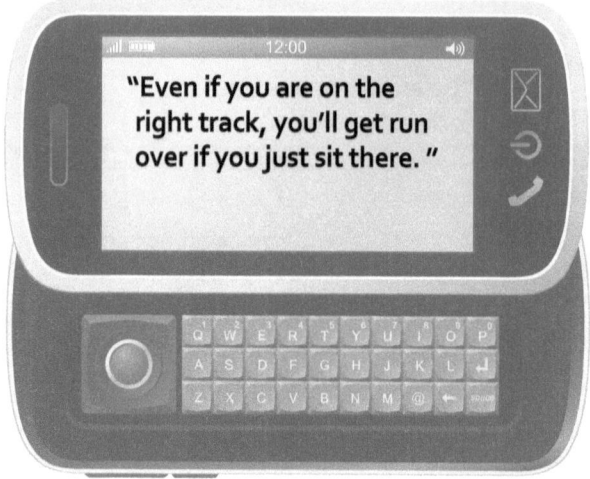

Will Rogers
Entertainer

 Getting started in the right place is just the beginning. Then you have to make something of it every day.

TEXTS 2 TEENS

Chapter 1: Actions

 Millions of people cannot function unless they are a small part of a larger group. They have no real ideas of their own, but borrow and add to the ideas of others.

TEXTS 2 TEENS

Sending the advice and wisdom that they desperately need

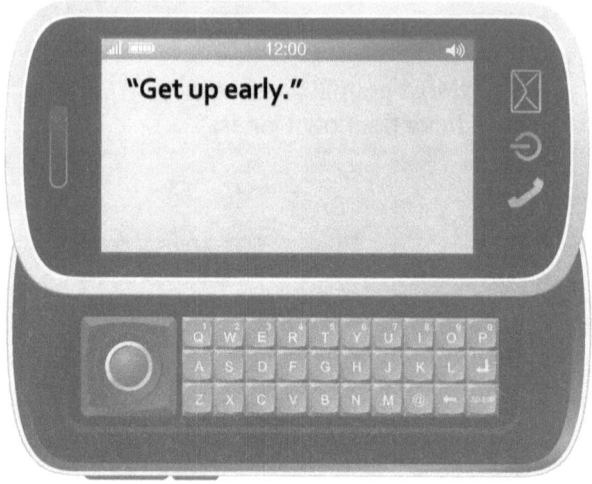

Maureen Sharib
Recruiter, TechTrack.com

There is a lot happening in the world and you miss half of it if you don't get out of bed.

TEXTS 2 TEENS

Chapter 1: Actions

Ron Sprikle
Senior Architect, SAIC

The hard things are the most rewarding. Once you have conquered something easy, do not keep doing it over an over. Move on to something bigger, better, and harder. It will be a thrill.

TEXTS 2 TEENS

Sending the advice and wisdom that they desperately need

John Mann
Senior Engineer, ARA

 Your goal is too low if you can accomplish it quickly and have nothing more to shoot for. Create a goal that will move you for years.

Chapter 2

ATTITUDE

TEXTS 2 TEENS

Sending the advice and wisdom that they desperately need

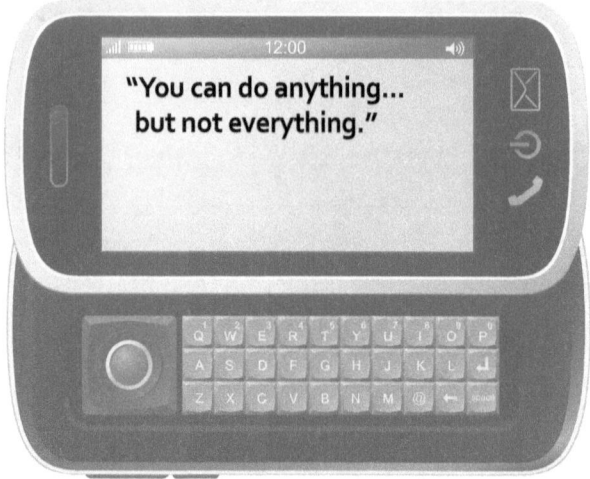

Bill Waite
*Chairman and CTO,
AEgis Technologies Group*

Bill is an incredibly diverse executive and technologist. But even he realizes that people have a limited amount of time and energy. We all have the talent to do anything we want, but none of us has the time and energy to do everything we can think of. Choose your most precious "anything" and do not let the ocean of "everything" overwhelm you.

TEXTS 2 TEENS

Chapter 2: Attitude

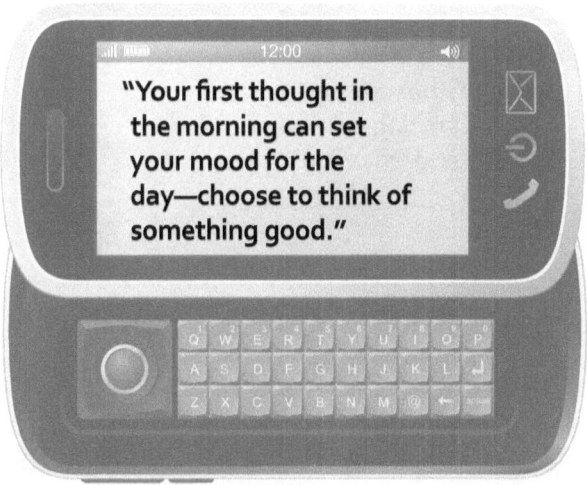

 Start your brain off on the right track every morning. Think about your blessings and the exciting things that lie ahead. Choose not to start with negative or depressing thoughts.

TEXTS 2 TEENS

Sending the advice and wisdom that they desperately need

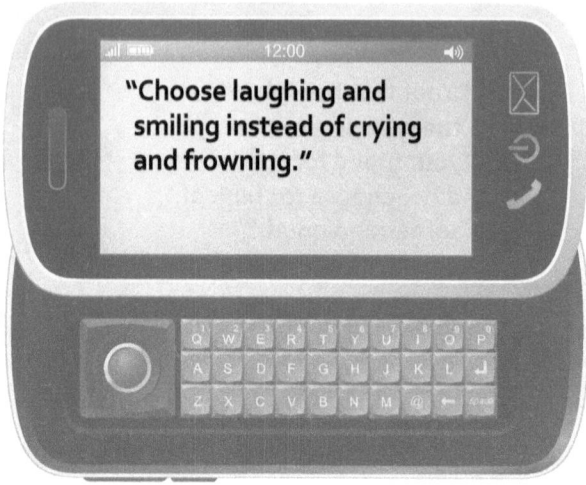

 You can laugh and smile on purpose. Do it and your mood will improve immediately.

TEXTS 2 TEENS

Chapter 2: Attitude

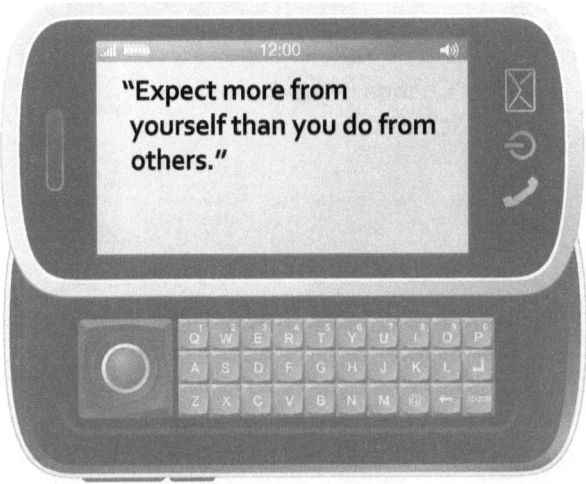

Dr. Ricardo Valerdi
MIT Research Associate

 Push yourself to accomplish great things.

TEXTS 2 TEENS

Sending the advice and wisdom that they desperately need

Carol Wideman
CEO, Vcom3D Inc

Life is change. Nothing is the same today as it was yesterday and tomorrow it will change again. Embrace change, cause change, don't avoid it.

TEXTS 2 TEENS

Chapter 2: Attitude

John Blair
Aviation Dispatcher, Boeing

 Fear is a giant cloud of vapor. It is made of nothing, but can stop you from seeing everything. Cut through your fear and discover what is on the other side.

TEXTS 2 TEENS

Sending the advice and wisdom that they desperately need

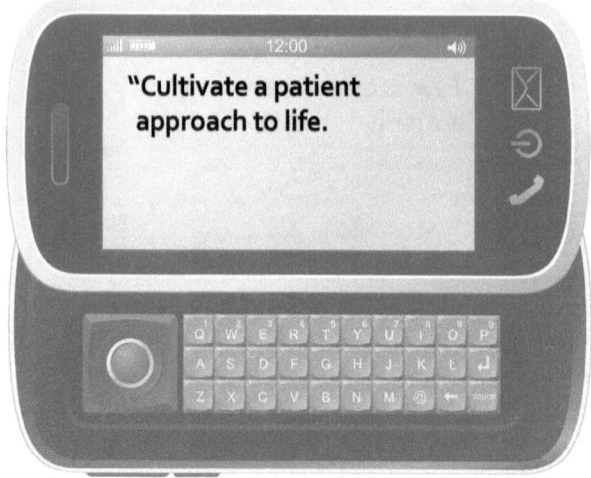

Eric Stierna
Colonel, US Army

 Our society is one of immediacy and instant gratification. Teaching yourself to be patient in all things will help you live with less stress, greater satisfaction, and a better chance for happiness.

TEXTS 2 TEENS

Chapter 2: Attitude

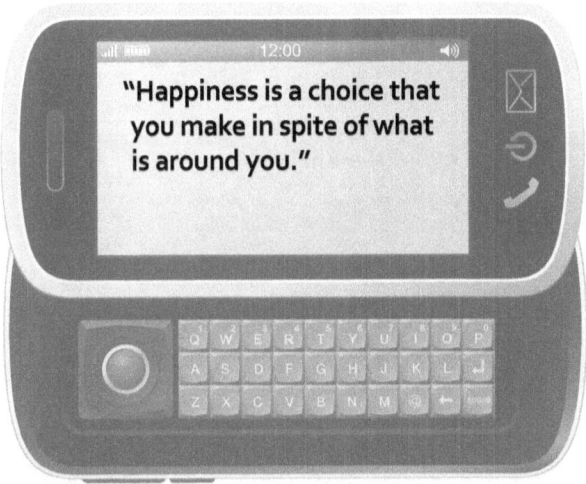

 Happiness comes from the inside. It is not caused from the outside. You can choose to be happy just by deciding to.

TEXTS 2 TEENS

Sending the advice and wisdom that they desperately need

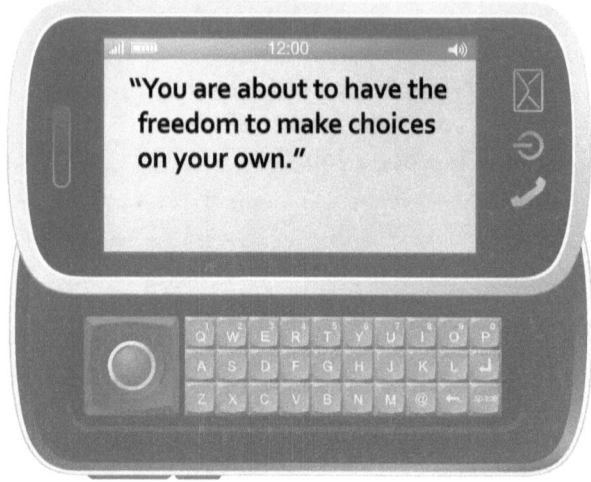

Gary Woods
*Engineering Manager,
General Dynamics*

Take five short seconds to think about the possible outcomes of your choices before you make them.

TEXTS 2 TEENS

Chapter 2: Attitude

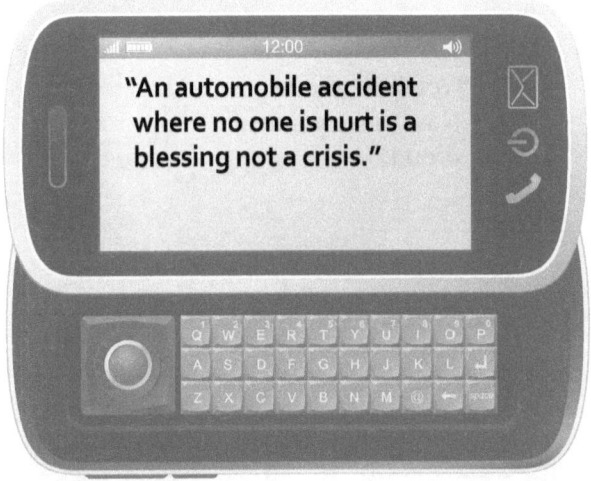

 We all have accidents eventually. If you come out unhurt, then it was a big deal for the car, but not for the humans.

TEXTS 2 TEENS

Sending the advice and wisdom that they desperately need

Scott Hopkins
Chief Engineer, SAIC

 Eventually you will judge your impact on the world based on your own internal expectations. Set your expectations high and work for your own approval.

TEXTS 2 TEENS

Chapter 2: Attitude

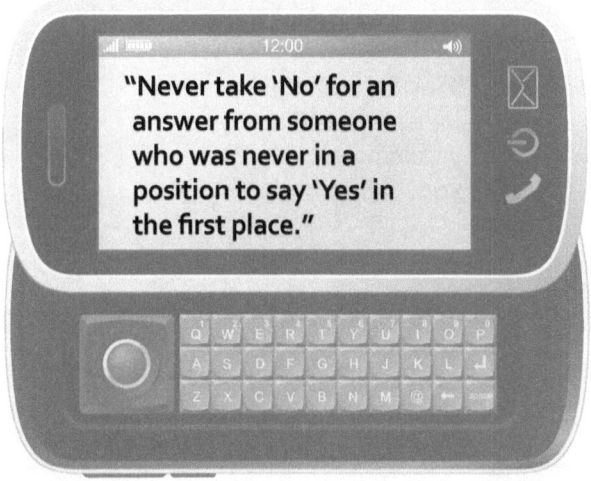

Scott Ariotti
Director Sales & Marketing, DiSTI

Most people who say "No" do not have the power to stop you or to help you. Do not let them hold you back.

TEXTS 2 TEENS

Sending the advice and wisdom that they desperately need

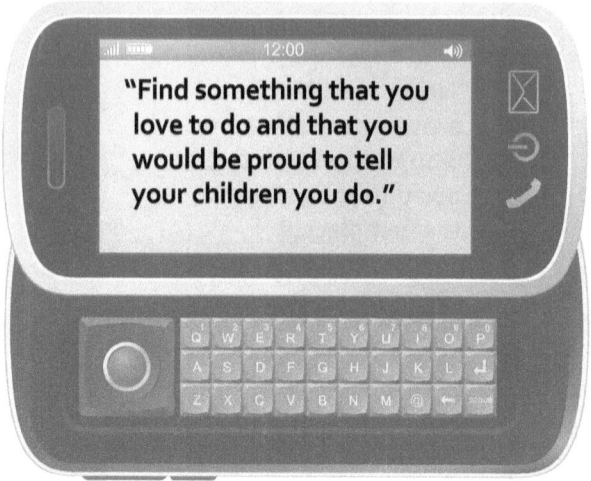

Jim Craig
Vice President, Lockheed Martin

If you do not love your job, it is hard to love your life. You can't spend a huge amount of time doing something you hate and still be able to love life.

TEXTS 2 TEENS

Chapter 2: Attitude

Lisa Galarneau
User Experience Researcher, Microsoft

In the 21st century we finally realize that perfection is impossible, but there is much more value in being unique.

TEXTS 2 TEENS

Sending the advice and wisdom that they desperately need

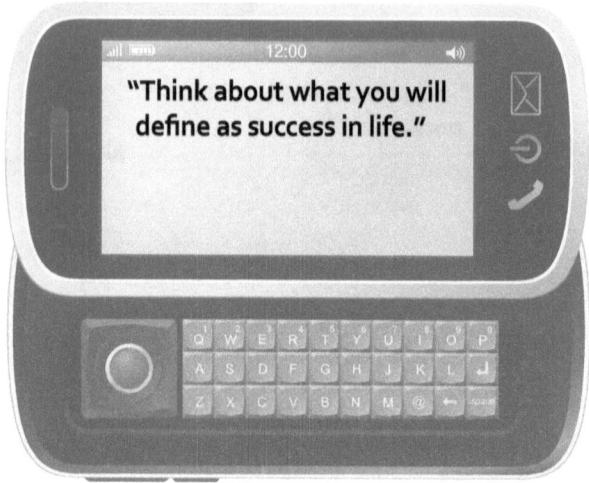

Rick Severinghaus
The AEgis Technologies Group

 Parents, family, and friends can help, but it is really only you who decides which life you will lead.

TEXTS 2 TEENS

Chapter 2: Attitude

Bill Nickels
Professor, University of Maryland

 Happiness is the ability to appreciate who you are, what you have, and your life as it is right now.

TEXTS 2 TEENS
Sending the advice and wisdom that they desperately need

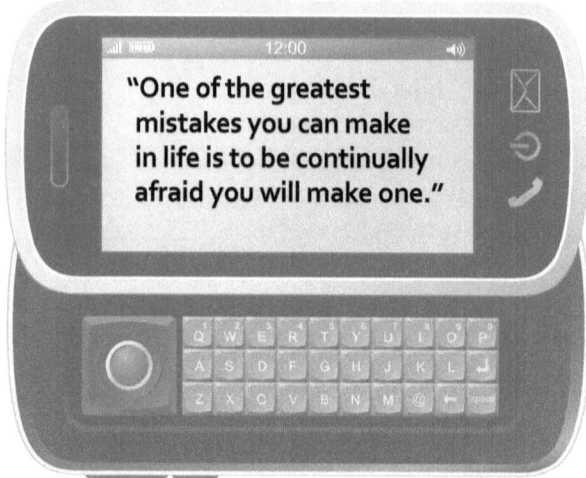

Robert H. Smith
Philanthropist

Fear can stop you from trying everything that is new. You should be more afraid of doing nothing at all.

TEXTS 2 TEENS

Chapter 2: Attitude

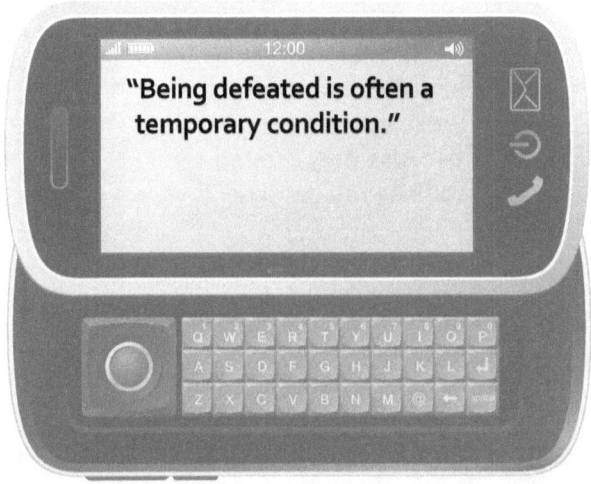

Robert H. Smith
Philanthropist

 Giving up is what makes it permanent.

TEXTS 2 TEENS

Sending the advice and wisdom that they desperately need

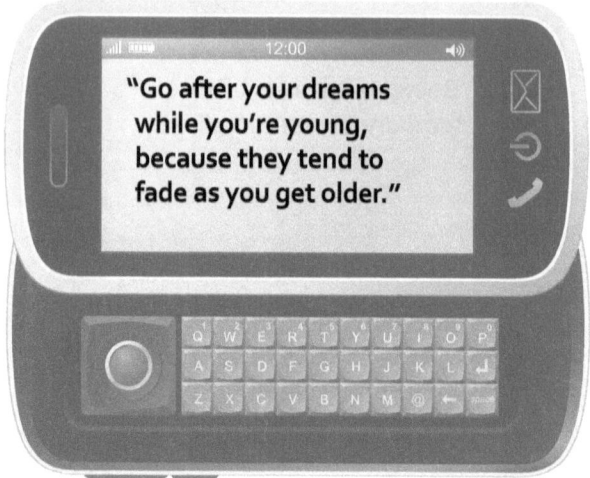

John Mann
Senior Engineer, ARA

 Do not wait to be old enough to pursue your dreams. You are already old enough to get started.

TEXTS 2 TEENS

Chapter 2: Attitude

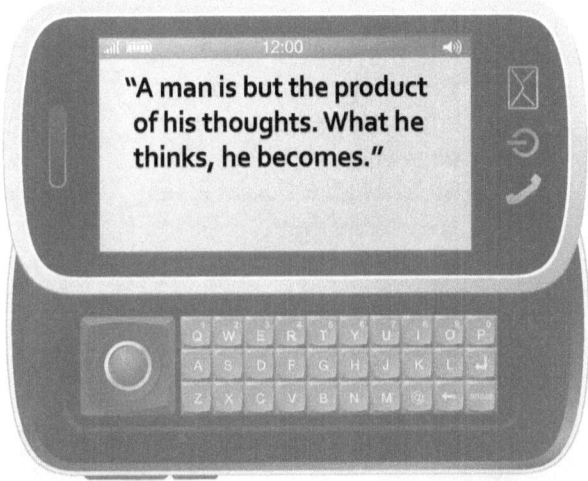

"A man is but the product of his thoughts. What he thinks, he becomes."

Gandhi
Indian Political Leader

 Your thoughts guide your actions, or inactions. Your actions are your life and your person. What you think controls who you become.

TEXTS 2 TEENS

Sending the advice and wisdom that they desperately need

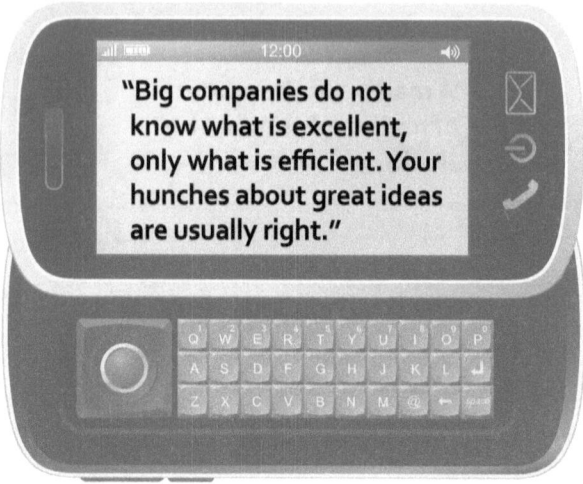

"Big companies do not know what is excellent, only what is efficient. Your hunches about great ideas are usually right."

 Bureaucracies do not paint masterpieces. They are great at doing everything average and nothing outstanding.

Chapter 2: Attitude

Ed Payne
*Senior Program Manager,
Lockheed Martin*

 Silence is underrated as a socialization skill. There are too many people talking and not enough people listening silently.

Chapter 3

CHARACTER

TEXTS 2 TEENS

Sending the advice and wisdom that they desperately need

 Friends, coworkers, husbands, and wives of good character are 100 times more valuable than those with good looks. This becomes much more obvious as you get older.

TEXTS 2 TEENS

Chapter 3: Character

 America has been so successful that we are now in an eternal pursuit of "more". There is no satisfactions on this path. Be happy with what you have and do not try to acquire every new thing that comes along.

TEXTS 2 TEENS

Sending the advice and wisdom that they desperately need

Colonel Chris Oliver
US Army

Your actions are part of who you are. They come from your own decisions. You are responsible for what you cause to happen in the world.

TEXTS 2 TEENS

Chapter 3: Character

Mark Friedman
Analyst,
Concurrent Technologies Corporation

 Always take the high road when given a reasonable choice.

TEXTS 2 TEENS
Sending the advice and wisdom that they desperately need

"If your actions reflect who you were at that point in time, that's a pretty good deal."

Kim Wright
COO, Stupid Fun Club Inc.

Be true to who you are now and proud of your dedication to it. You will grow and change over the years, but you will leave a trail of honesty behind you.

TEXTS 2 TEENS

Chapter 3: Character

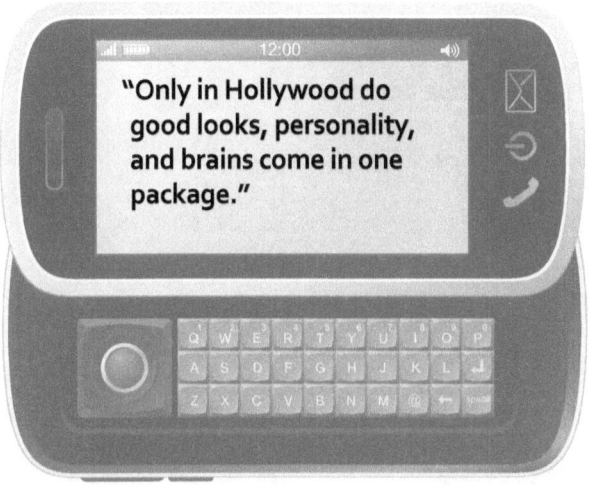

 And only in Hollywood is someone looking for friends and partners who must have all of them.

TEXTS 2 TEENS

Sending the advice and wisdom that they desperately need

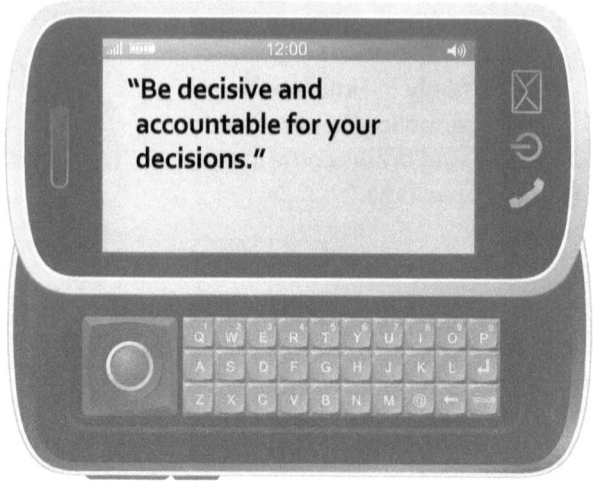

Rich Gombos
*Senior Systems Engineer,
Cole Engineering*

 Remember, wisdom is the application of knowledge gained from having chosen poorly.

Chapter 3: Character

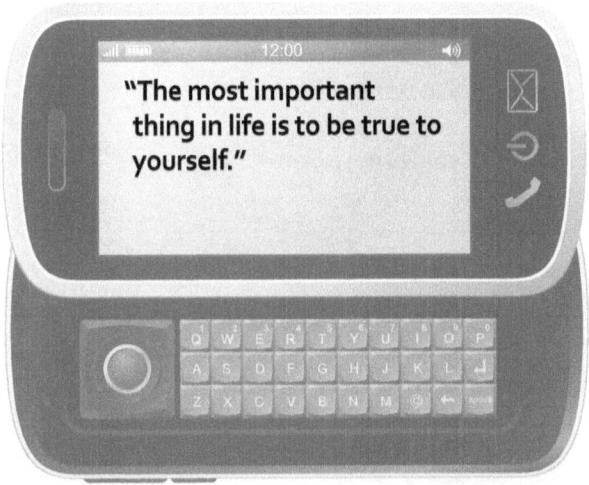

Gregg Hamilton
Senior Software Engineer, Symantec

Shakespeare's plays were full of people who could not live with themselves after betraying who they really were.

TEXTS 2 TEENS

Sending the advice and wisdom that they desperately need

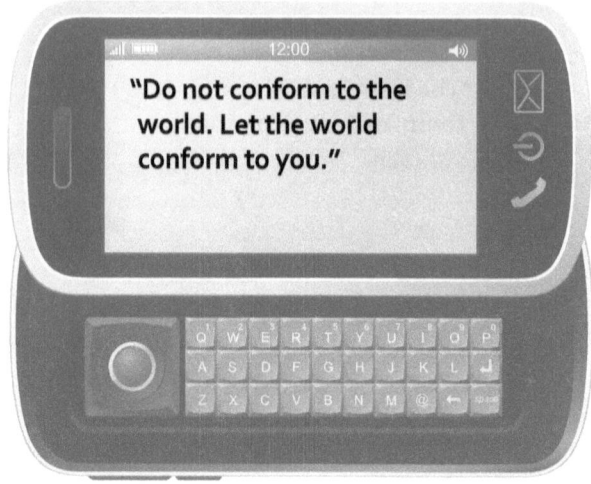

Jay Riggins
Program Manager,
L-3 Communications

There is not an empty place in the world shaped just like you are shaped. You have to make that hole yourself. If you don't, then you will have to shape yourself into someone else's hole.

TEXTS 2 TEENS

Chapter 3: Character

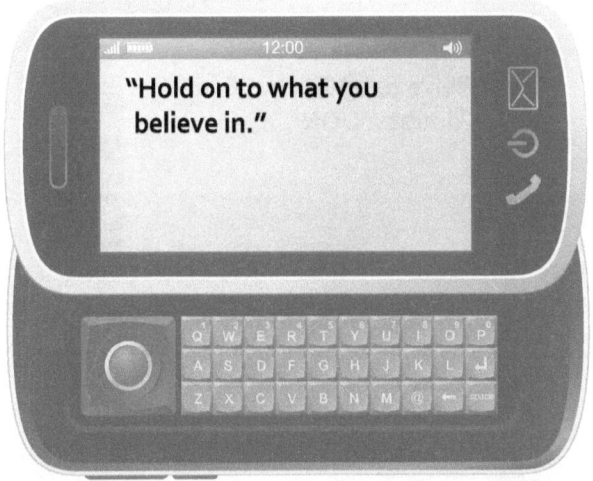

Philippe Geril
*Secretary General,
EUROSIS*

Do not betray yourself because you will always remember and regret it.

TEXTS 2 TEENS
Sending the advice and wisdom that they desperately need

Graham Whiteside
General Manager, Limbs & Things

 Make the most of the life you have. But do not take it too far. You can sail over the edge of the world and never get back.

Chapter 3: Character

"A big shot is just a little shot that kept on shooting."

Zig Ziglar
Author & Speaker

You do not become an expert in one try. Just keep working at what you love, you will become excellent with time.

TEXTS 2 TEENS

Sending the advice and wisdom that they desperately need

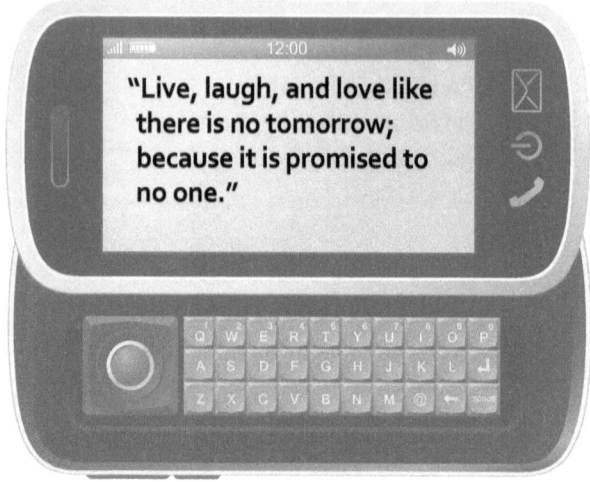

Vaughn Bullard
CEO, Bullard Acquisitions

 Never put off for tomorrow the life you want to live today.

TEXTS 2 TEENS

Chapter 3: Character

Chris Giordano
Director, DiSTI Corporation

 If I've done my job as a parent, then you will do just fine.

TEXTS 2 TEENS

Sending the advice and wisdom that they desperately need

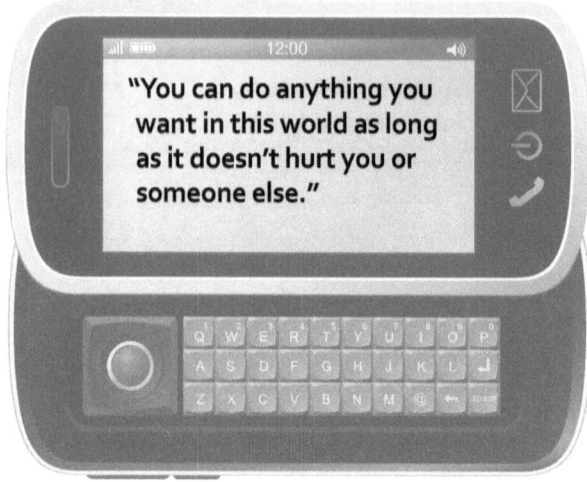

Bob Sottilare
*Chief Technology Officer,
US Army RDECOM*

 That is a pretty big license for experiencing life. Do not destroy people and the rest is up for grabs.

Chapter 3: Character

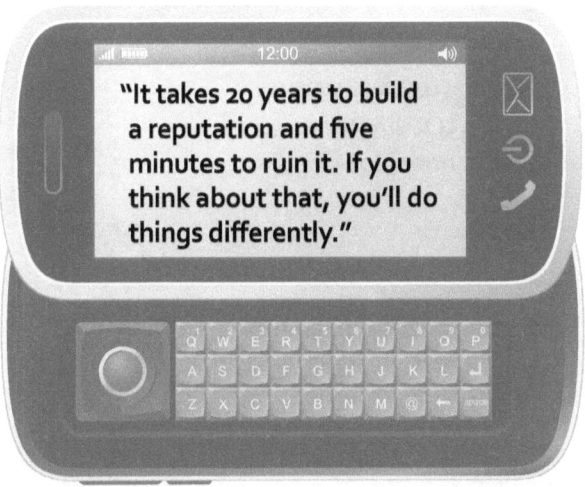

"It takes 20 years to build a reputation and five minutes to ruin it. If you think about that, you'll do things differently."

Warren Buffett
Investor

 Do not take a good reputation for granted. Good ones are hard to build, easy to lose, and almost impossible to regain.

TEXTS 2 TEENS

Sending the advice and wisdom that they desperately need

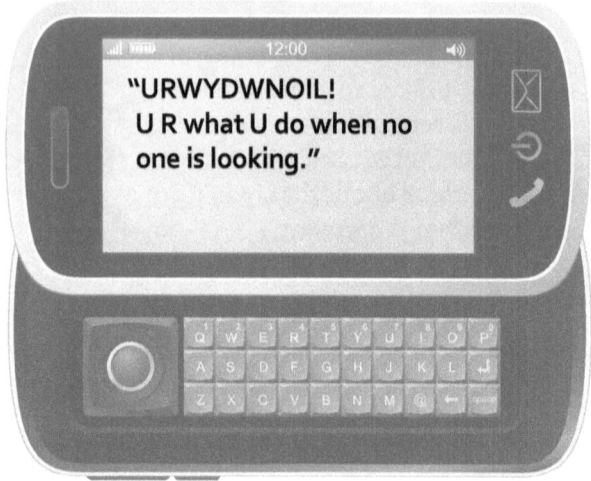

Steve Griffith
Director, Objective Interface Systems

 Even though no one sees your actions, they do affect what you become and where you end up.

Chapter 4

CONFIDENCE

TEXTS 2 TEENS

Sending the advice and wisdom that they desperately need

Marco Pluijm
Manager, Amsterdam Port Authority

 Don't give up being who you really are because you believe that all successful people conform to some sterile standard. They don't.

TEXTS 2 TEENS

Chapter 4: Confidence

Jon Watte
Engineering Director, IMVU

Risk is wonderful and thrilling if you can afford to lose what you have wagered. But do not risk more than you can afford to lose.

TEXTS 2 TEENS

Sending the advice and wisdom that they desperately need

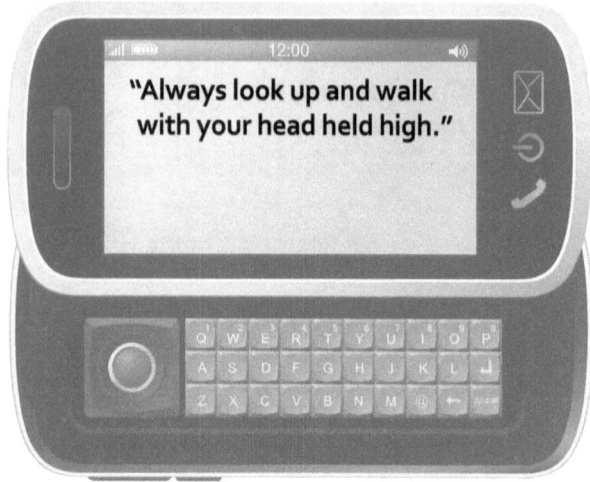

Dr. Elaine Rayburn
Scientist, Sandia National Labs

You can be proud of what you have done, where you are headed, and the good you have added to the world. Hold onto that pride and show it in your approach to the world.

TEXTS 2 TEENS

Chapter 4: Confidence

Stella Aquilina
Senior Software Engineer,
L-3 Communications

The world is full of monsters trying to scare you away from your joy and excitement. Don't get off the boogie board for the monsters.

TEXTS 2 TEENS

Sending the advice and wisdom that they desperately need

John McElver
Software Executive

You'll never make a mistake that I haven't already made. You will learn far more from your mistakes than you ever will from your successes.

TEXTS 2 TEENS

Chapter 4: Confidence

 Red fear moves you away from danger. Blue fear moves you away from adventure, opportunity, and the unknown. You have to learn to tell the difference between the two.

TEXTS 2 TEENS

Sending the advice and wisdom that they desperately need

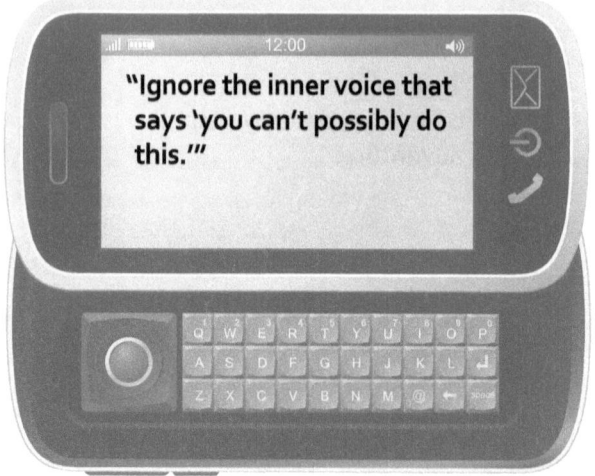

Buck Leahy
Consultant

The voice of fear lives inside of everyone. Listening to it leads to failure, overcoming it leads to greatness.

TEXTS 2 TEENS

Chapter 4: Confidence

Debbie Dyson
Director of Exhibits, NTSA

 Teenagers spend way too much time allowing negative thoughts to create who they are rather than embracing positive thoughts and becoming as great as they can be.

Chapter 5

EDUCATION

TEXTS 2 TEENS

Sending the advice and wisdom that they desperately need

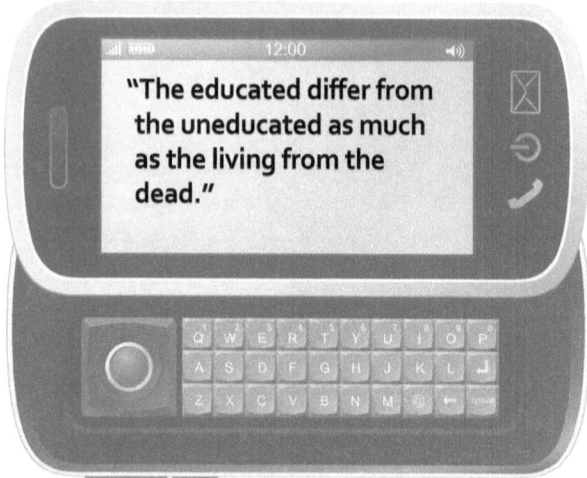

"The educated differ from the uneducated as much as the living from the dead."

Aristotle
Philosopher

Even 2,300 years ago Aristotle could see the fundamental impact that education has on people and a population. He knew that the progress of humankind was more dependent upon education than hard work. Working hard at the same things you did yesterday will keep the organization running just like it ran yesterday. But moving forward requires learning, education, and new knowledge.

Chapter 5: Education

Dr. Katherine Morse
Senior Staff,
Johns Hopkins University

History, society, and technology are built on the works of people who wrote their ideas down. Many more ideas were lost because the creator did not commit them to paper. Years or centuries past before those ideas were rediscovered by someone who made them a permanent part of history by writing them down.

TEXTS 2 TEENS

Sending the advice and wisdom that they desperately need

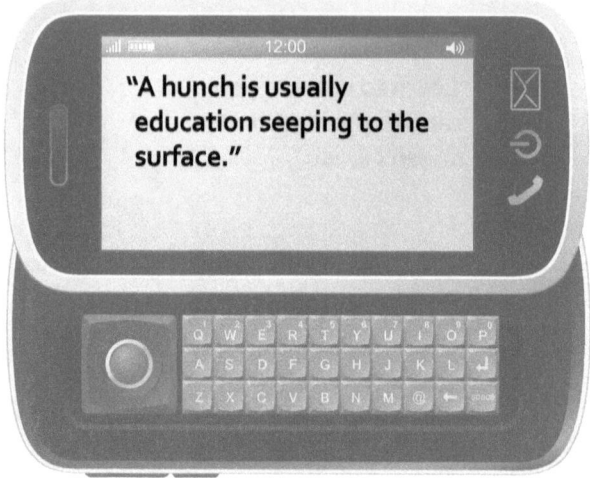

 All of the knowledge and experience that you accumulate forms a deep pool that your brain uses to understand the world around you.

TEXTS 2 TEENS

Chapter 5: Education

Everything that you do is based on what you have learned. Education comes in hundreds of different forms, accept all of it that you can.

TEXTS 2 TEENS

Sending the advice and wisdom that they desperately need

 Learning by personal experience or by trial and error can be extremely expensive. Whenever possible learn from others rather than from experience.

TEXTS 2 TEENS

Chapter 5: Education

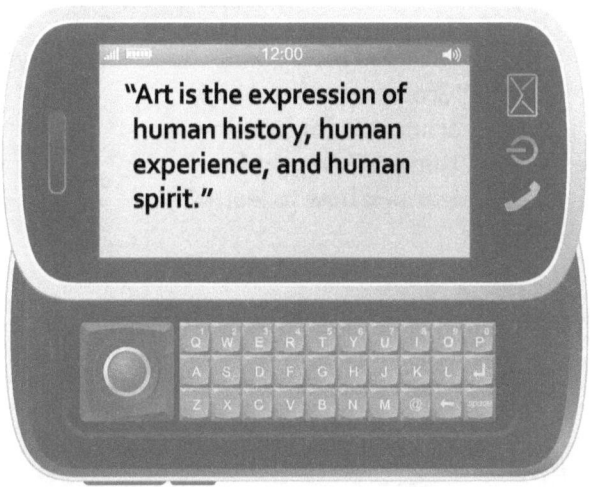

 A painting, vase, or building is an expression of the human spirit. All of them are an attempt to express the richness of what it means to be human.

TEXTS 2 TEENS

Sending the advice and wisdom that they desperately need

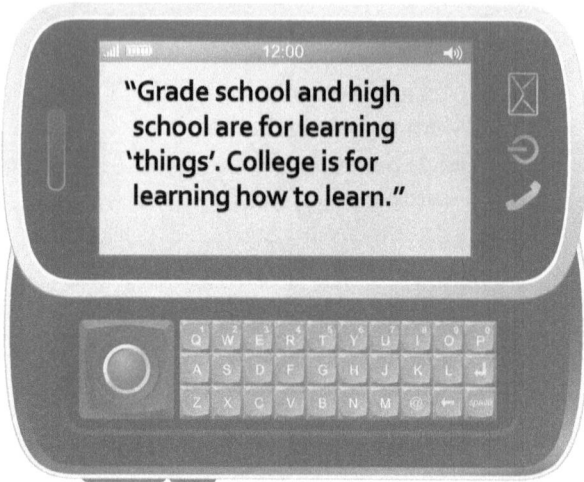

Peter Lattimore
Chief Scientist, RhinoCorps

 College is for building confidence in yourself so that you can adapt as times change because you know how to learn.

TEXTS 2 TEENS

Chapter 5: Education

André Correia
Structural Engineer, Portugal

 If your parents did not handle life successfully, you would not be here. Your very existence is proof that your parents have something to teach you.

TEXTS 2 TEENS

Sending the advice and wisdom that they desperately need

Vincent Vanderbent
Project Manager, New York City

 The hunch in your gut is often based on a huge pool of knowledge and experience that you cannot completely understand.

TEXTS 2 TEENS

Chapter 5: Education

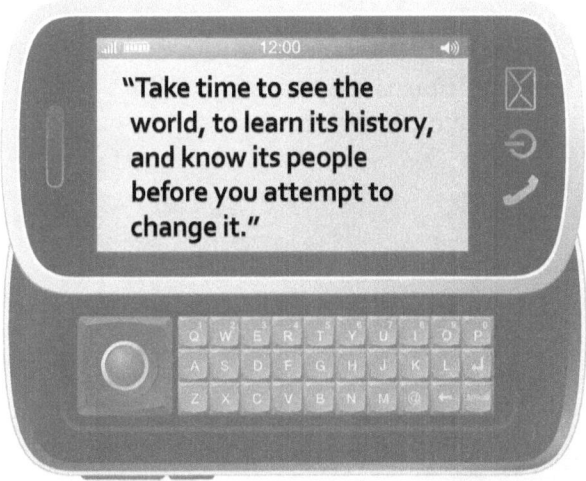

Don Chaney
Captain, US Navy

The world is an amazing and beautiful place. Take the time to see it and understand it. It will show you parts of yourself that you did not know existed.

TEXTS 2 TEENS

Sending the advice and wisdom that they desperately need

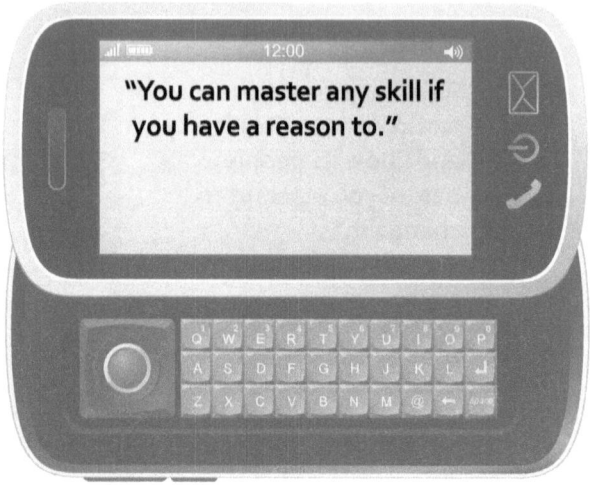

People learn to do amazing things because they have to and because they are driven to. Do not think that anything is beyond you if you really need it.

TEXTS 2 TEENS

Chapter 5: Education

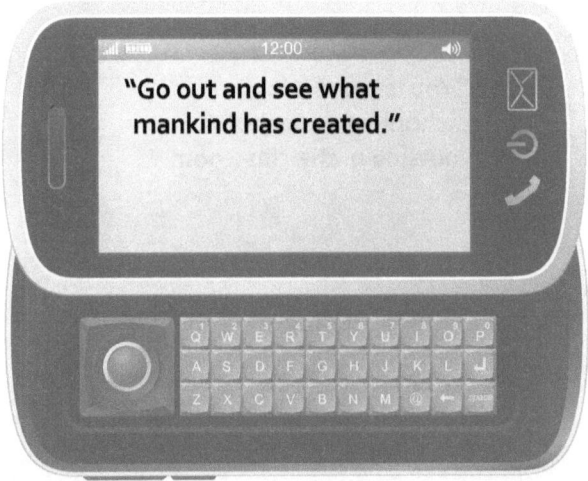

 There are more than seven wonders of the world. Every country and every city contains amazing accomplishments by the people who came before you.

TEXTS 2 TEENS

Sending the advice and wisdom that they desperately need

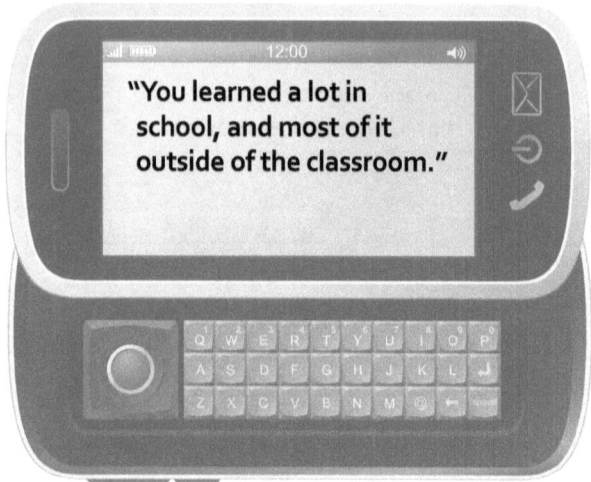

 You did not get a grade for everything that happened at recess, in the lunch room, and on the way home from school. But you learned a great deal that you will never forget and that you will use for a lifetime.

TEXTS 2 TEENS

Chapter 5: Education

Anita Bonner
Program Manager, AT&T

You never know where life will take you or what you might discover that you are interested in. It would be unfortunate to not be able to do something just because you wouldn't learn or put in a little extra effort.

TEXTS 2 TEENS

Sending the advice and wisdom that they desperately need

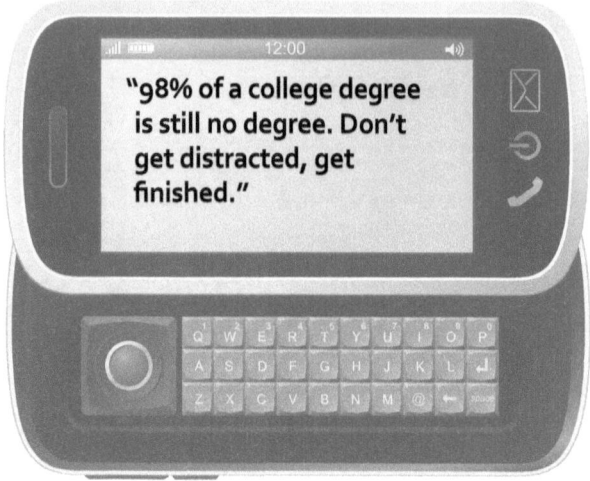

Mark Phillips
Vice President, MASA Group

College is not like painting a house. If you don't finish then the world does not care how close you almost came, it is the same as not doing it at all.

TEXTS 2 TEENS

Chapter 5: Education

Jack Gruninger
President, TapHere! Technology

 There is a good reason that Proverbs has persisted as a leading source of wisdom for almost three thousand years. Dig in and find out why it is so valuable.

TEXTS 2 TEENS

Sending the advice and wisdom that they desperately need

Stephanie Graffuis
Sr. Software Engineer, StackFrame

 College and business are still formally correct where you have to talk and write like an intelligent person.

Chapter 5: Education

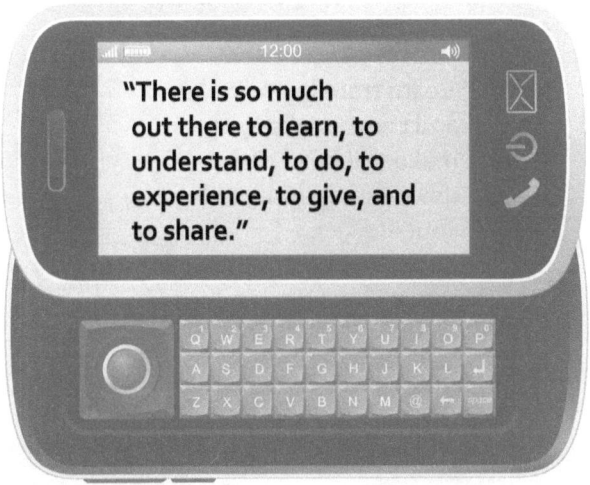

Brian Bilick
Sales Manager, VT MAK

 Enrich your life with all there is to experience.

TEXTS 2 TEENS

Sending the advice and wisdom that they desperately need

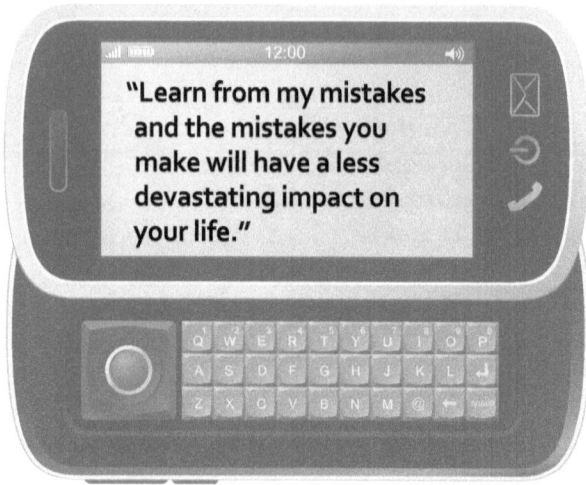

Steve Hunnell
Configuration Manager, SAIC

Society moves forward specifically because we all learn from those who came before us. Not learning is a way of moving backward.

Chapter 5: Education

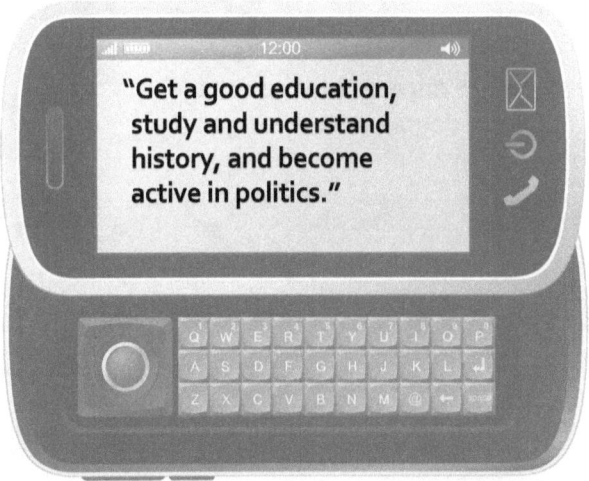

Jay Roland
Rolands & Associates

The more you understand the world, the more you will want to improve it. In sprite of the reputation of politics, it really is one of the best ways to improve the lives of the people in a country.

TEXTS 2 TEENS

Sending the advice and wisdom that they desperately need

"You are not your college degree or your last job."

 You have brains and talent that can go in one hundred directions. Don't be afraid to jump into something new.

TEXTS 2 TEENS

Chapter 5: Education

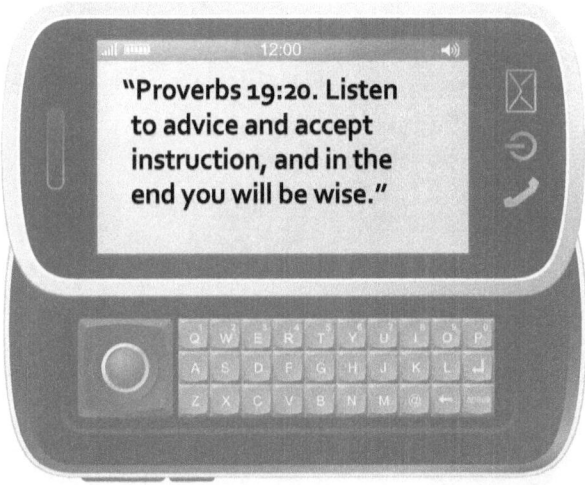

Wayne Lindo
*Senior Systems Engineer,
DEI Services*

Taking advice does not mean you are stupid or wrong, it means you have not learned everything yet. You can become wise through the experience of others.

TEXTS 2 TEENS

Sending the advice and wisdom that they desperately need

Seth Godin
Author

School is meant to prepare you for life, not to prepare you for more school. The real world is bigger, wilder, and more chaotic than anything in school. Learn to be good at life, not just good at school.

TEXTS 2 TEENS

Chapter 5: Education

Dr. Margaret Loper
Professor, Georgia Tech

There are plenty of people that can help you when you have a problem and plenty that you can help as well. Team up with some of them.

TEXTS 2 TEENS
Sending the advice and wisdom that they desperately need

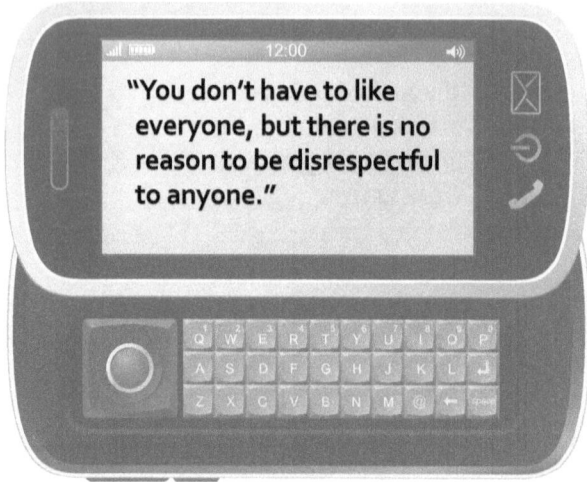

Dr. Margaret Loper
Professor, Georgia Tech

Treating people with respect and courtesy is not determined by whether you like them, but by the kind of person that you are.

Chapter 6

JOY

TEXTS 2 TEENS

Sending the advice and wisdom that they desperately need

Perry Geib

 We all believe in hard work. But we also believe in enjoying every day that we have.

TEXTS 2 TEENS

Chapter 6: Joy

Phillip Skiffington
Account Manager, MISource

 If you focus on the positives in life rather than the negatives it's makes life a lot simpler.

TEXTS 2 TEENS

Sending the advice and wisdom that they desperately need

Janet Williams
Director of Software Development, Milum Corp.

 You will be an adult for a loooong time, so just enjoy the journey.

Chapter 6: Joy

Linda LoCicero
*Operations Manager,
The Staffing Company*

Too soon you'll be a grown up with grown up worries. Enjoy each moment as it happens.

TEXTS 2 TEENS

Sending the advice and wisdom that they desperately need

 Teenagers live on their emotions and their hormones. The real world does not. If you indulge your temper tantrums, then you will be locked out of the real world.

Chapter 6: Joy

Andy Smith
Owner, Halldale Media

21st century intensity at work sometimes makes us forget to enjoy the rich world that we have already built. If you can't enjoy it, there is no reason to build it.

TEXTS 2 TEENS

Sending the advice and wisdom that they desperately need

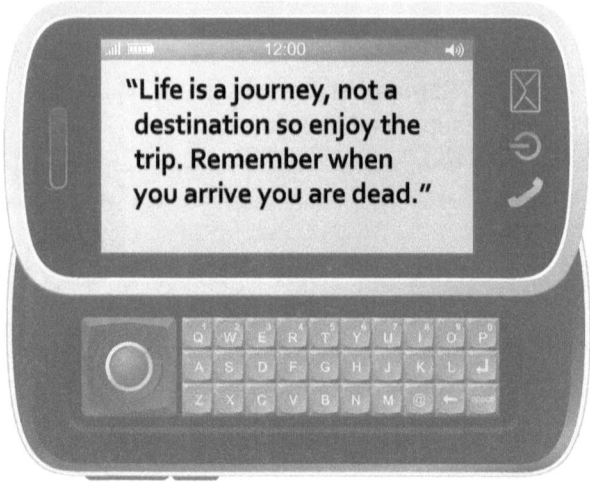

Mark Herbert
*Associate Partner,
Edwards Executive Search*

 Do not start living "someday". Start living today. The starting line for life is not someplace or sometime ahead of you, it is already behind you.

Chapter 7

LOVE

TEXTS 2 TEENS

Sending the advice and wisdom that they desperately need

David Flanagan
Consultant

Parents love you through the good and the bad. They are dedicated to you, not to what you do.

TEXTS 2 TEENS

Chapter 7: Love

 Pets let you practice expressing love. They give you a "love workout".

TEXTS 2 TEENS

Sending the advice and wisdom that they desperately need

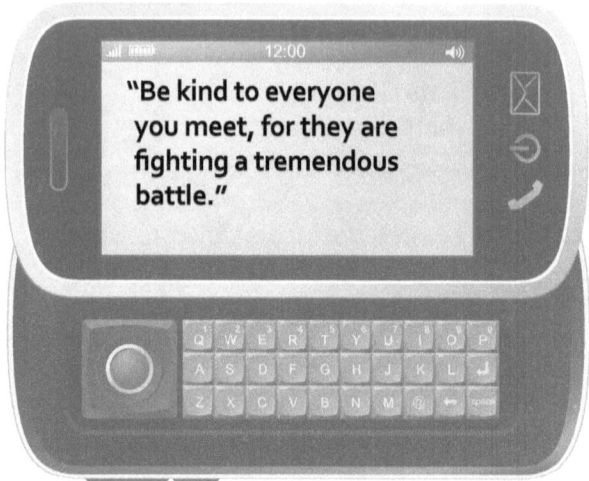

Chris Hawkins
Director of Sales,
AEgis Technologies Group

It is not always obvious, but everyone is wrestling with the same issues you have. Some of them are at a critical point and you just cannot see it on the surface. Try to help them through it in some small way.

TEXTS 2 TEENS

Chapter 7: Love

Lisa Galarneau
User Experience Researcher, Microsoft

Do not keep secret one of the most powerful forces in the world. Share it and let it strengthen the people that you care about.

TEXTS 2 TEENS

Sending the advice and wisdom that they desperately need

Lisa Galarneau
User Experience Researcher, Microsoft

You can really make a difference in people's lives. The younger they are the more your actions will effect them.

TEXTS 2 TEENS

Chapter 7: Love

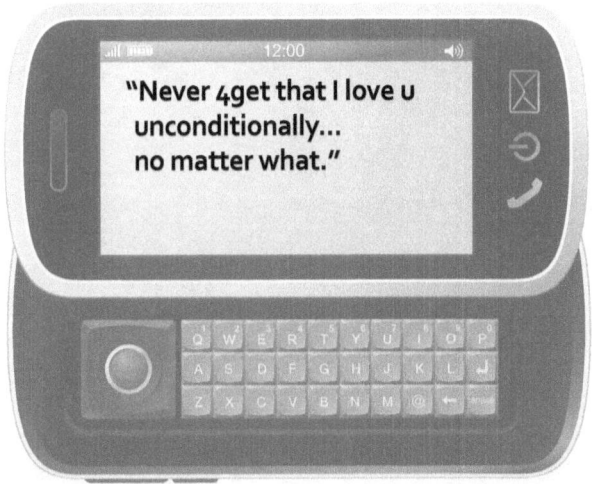

Dr. Lee Lacy
*Director,
Dynamics Research Corporation*

Parents will always be there for you. Do not doubt their devotion and support.

Chapter 8

RELATIONSHIPS

TEXTS 2 TEENS

Sending the advice and wisdom that they desperately need

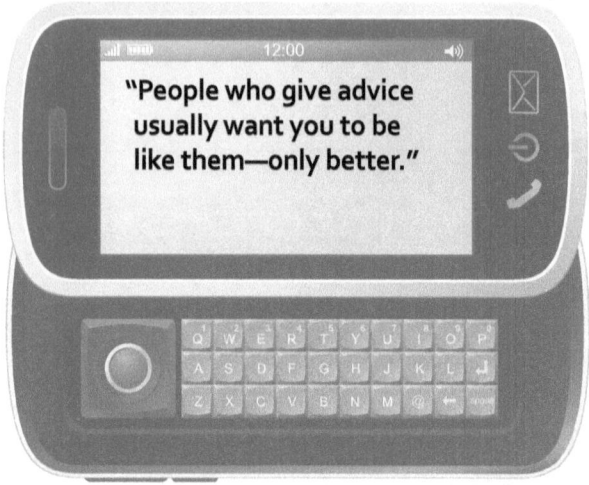

 Take advice from people that you admire and want to imitate. People only have advice from their own experience.

TEXTS 2 TEENS

Chapter 8: Relationships

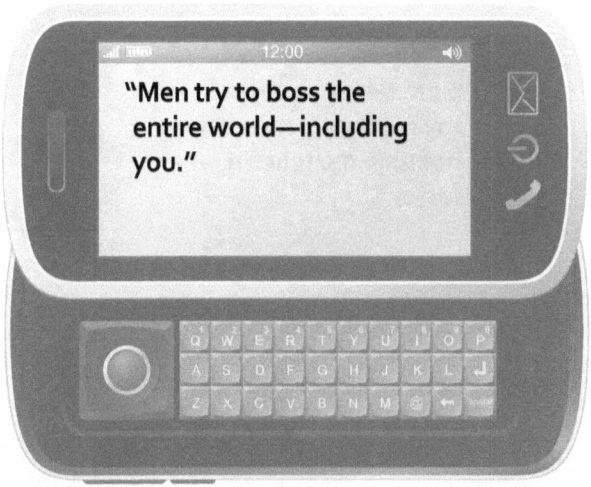

 Daughter, your boyfriend or husband was born and raised with the idea that he rules the world. He will also try to rule you. Balancing leadership and partnership is a constant challenge for him.

TEXTS 2 TEENS

Sending the advice and wisdom that they desperately need

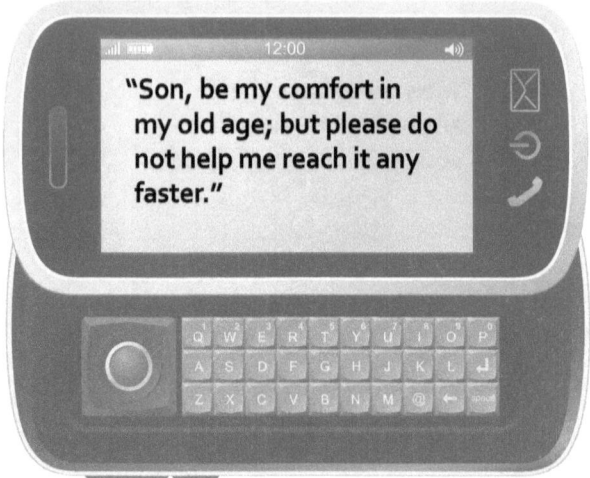

Abdul Hasan
Awal Dairy, Bahrain

There is nothing more wonderful than a son or daughter, and nothing with more power to make a parent old. Try not to put us in the grave any earlier than we need to be there.

TEXTS 2 TEENS

Chapter 8: Relationships

Michael Raines
President, 3D Perception

 It's not about driving a car, it's about life. Don't get mad. Recognize that others also have lives going on. It's not all about you. Breathe.

TEXTS 2 TEENS

Sending the advice and wisdom that they desperately need

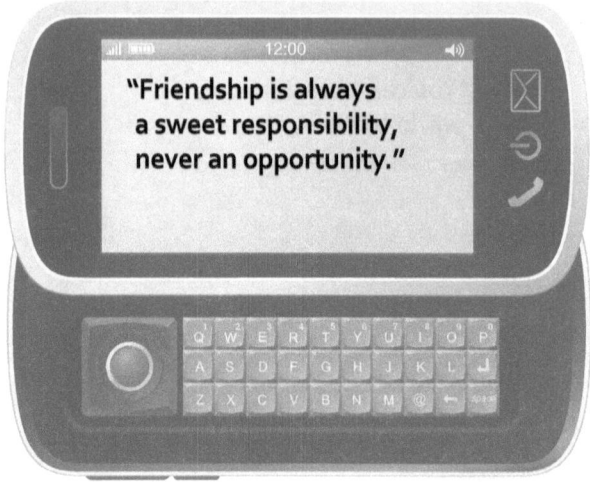

John Blair
Aviation Dispatcher, Boeing

Do not use your friends like you use toilet paper. They are one of the most valuable things you will ever have in life.

Chapter 8: Relationships

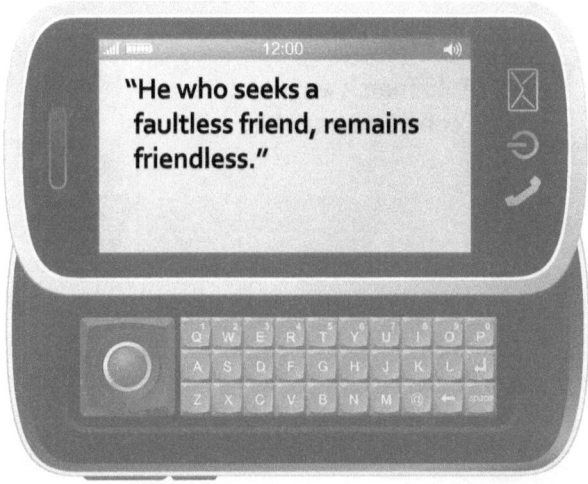

John Blair
Aviation Dispatcher, Boeing

You will never find a perfect friend—and you will never be a perfect friend. The flaws are what make friends so unique and valuable.

TEXTS 2 TEENS

Sending the advice and wisdom that they desperately need

John Donne
Author

 All humans are connected to each other. You support others and others support you.

Chapter 8: Relationships

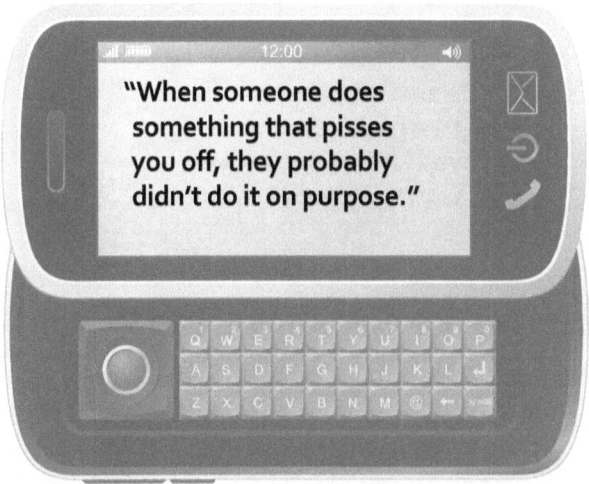

"When someone does something that pisses you off, they probably didn't do it on purpose."

Scott Messinger
*Applications Analyst,
Atmos Energy*

Give them more than one chance to show what kind of person they are. We all have a bad day or a terrible moment.

TEXTS 2 TEENS

Sending the advice and wisdom that they desperately need

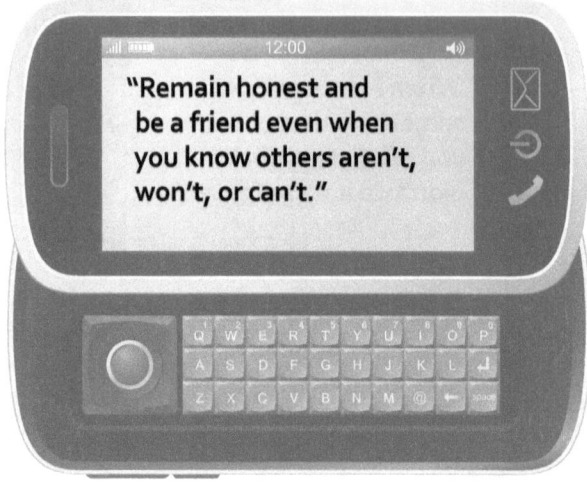

Dave Staats
Headhunter, SearchPartner

 The general benefit is worth the occasional disappointment. I wish I had started this at your age.

TEXTS 2 TEENS

Chapter 8: Relationships

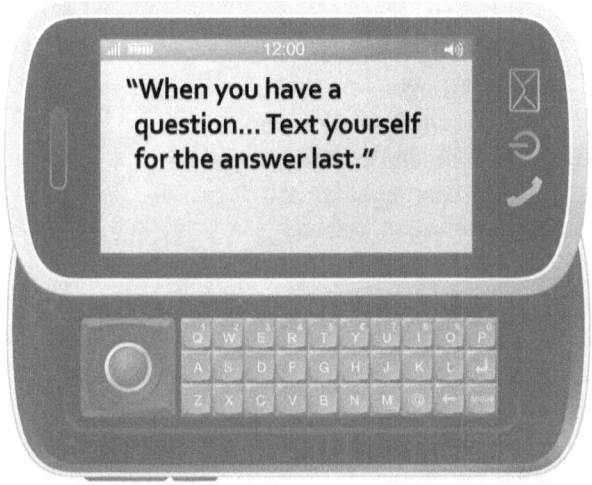

Brian Fields
President, L&N Fields

 Look for answers from other people before you turn to yourself. If you already knew the answer, then it wouldn't be a question.

TEXTS 2 TEENS

Sending the advice and wisdom that they desperately need

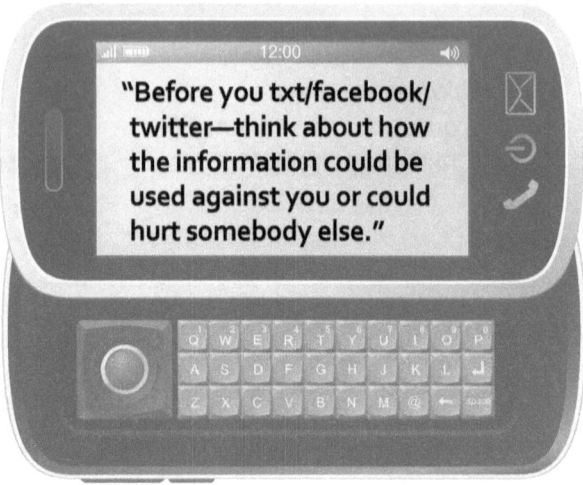

"Before you txt/facebook/twitter—think about how the information could be used against you or could hurt somebody else."

Remi Arnaud
*Chief Architect,
ScreamPoint International*

The information you release on the Internet can last forever and carry itself around the world.

TEXTS 2 TEENS

Chapter 8: Relationships

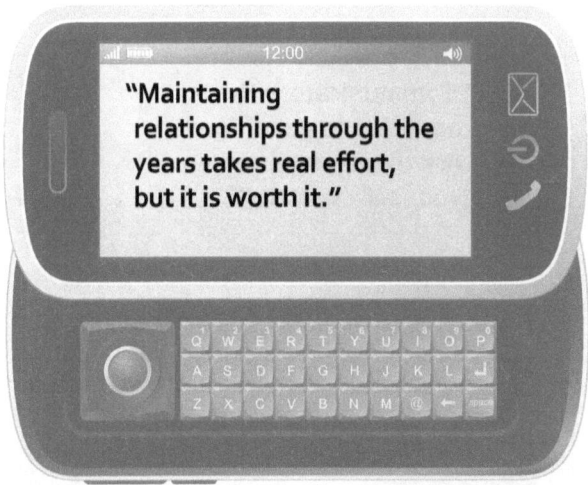

Hugh Henry
Engineering Lead,
MITRE Corporation

 Relationships are guaranteed to grow in value as you hold them longer. Like financial investments, they start small but can grow huge.

TEXTS 2 TEENS

Sending the advice and wisdom that they desperately need

Skip Songy
Program Manager, Sparta

 You do not have to tackle every problem on your own. Your family and friends can help you with ideas, energy, support, encouragement, and even money.

TEXTS 2 TEENS

Chapter 8: Relationships

Mike Daconta
*Chief Technology Officer,
Accelerated Information Management*

 Technology should always play second fiddle to real life. So, let's meet for lunch—my treat.

TEXTS 2 TEENS
Sending the advice and wisdom that they desperately need

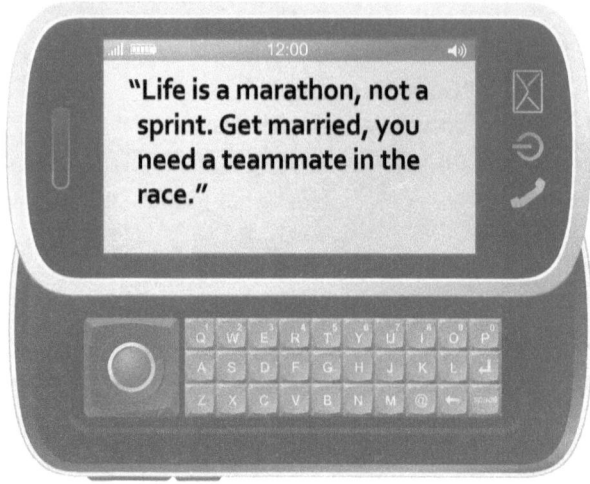

"Life is a marathon, not a sprint. Get married, you need a teammate in the race."

Dr. Mike Macedonia
Vice President, SAIC

 Do not try to tackle the world alone.

TEXTS 2 TEENS

Chapter 8: Relationships

Warren Buffett
Investor

 Pick out associates whose behavior is better than yours and you'll drift in that direction.

Chapter 9

WORK

TEXTS 2 TEENS
Sending the advice and wisdom that they desperately need

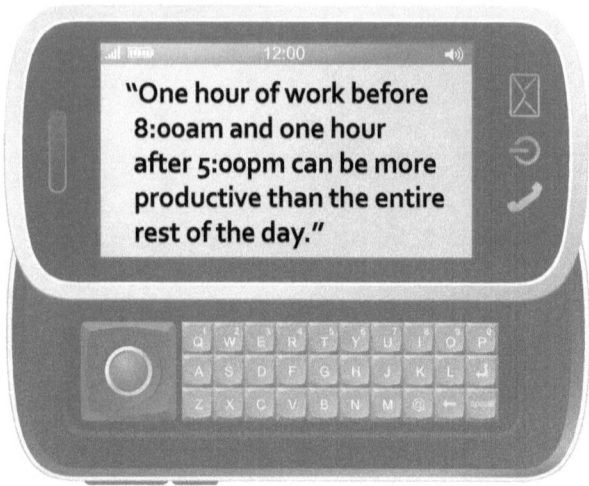

"One hour of work before 8:00am and one hour after 5:00pm can be more productive than the entire rest of the day."

 99% of the world works 8-to-5. They never know the productivity of working when everyone else is gone. They also miss the fraternity of those who arrive early and leave late.

TEXTS 2 TEENS

Chapter 9: Work

 Bureaucracy was created to make complex organizations and activities repeatable. It does not create excellence, it creates reliability. You cannot avoid it, but you have use it and still maintain your individuality.

TEXTS 2 TEENS

Sending the advice and wisdom that they desperately need

 There is no such thing as a big system that is run by a loose group of individuals. Big systems require big bureaucracies to keep them running year after year.

TEXTS 2 TEENS

Chapter 9: Work

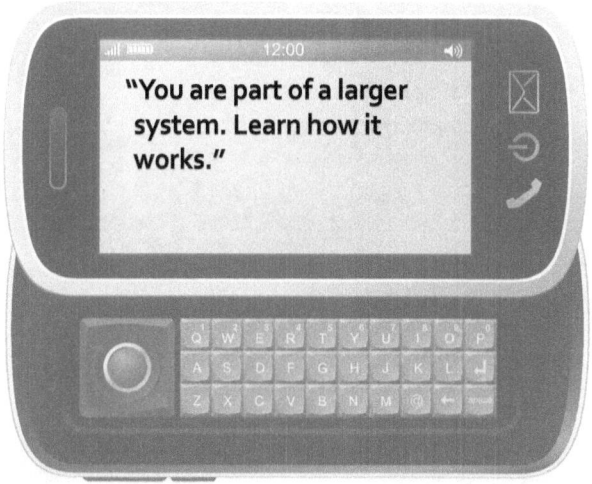

"You are part of a larger system. Learn how it works."

Big systems are fascinating. When you are inside of one, do not stick to your own little piece. Go through the whole system and see how it works.

TEXTS 2 TEENS

Sending the advice and wisdom that they desperately need

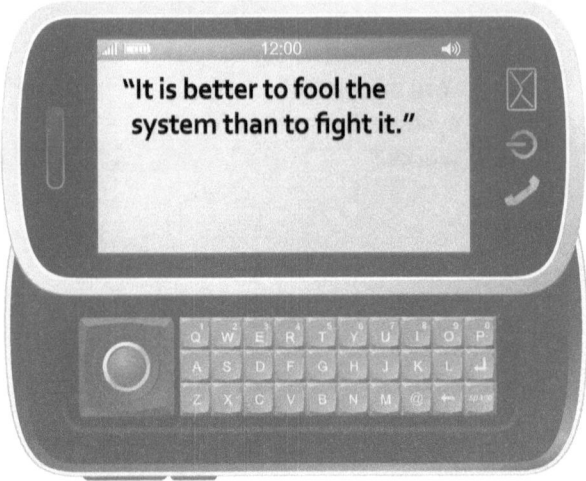

 Big systems are an unstoppable force. Do not fight them head-to-head. Instead deceive them and slide around them.

TEXTS 2 TEENS

Chapter 9: Work

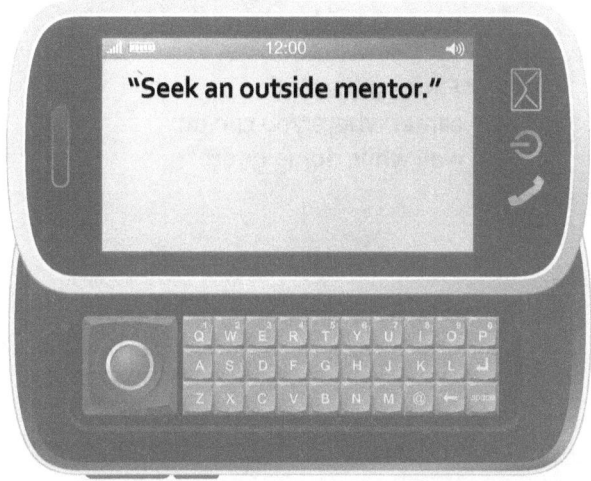

Stephen Day
CEO, Corporate Fission

 For some reason children cannot hear their parents, but the same words from a mentor are crystal clear.

TEXTS 2 TEENS

Sending the advice and wisdom that they desperately need

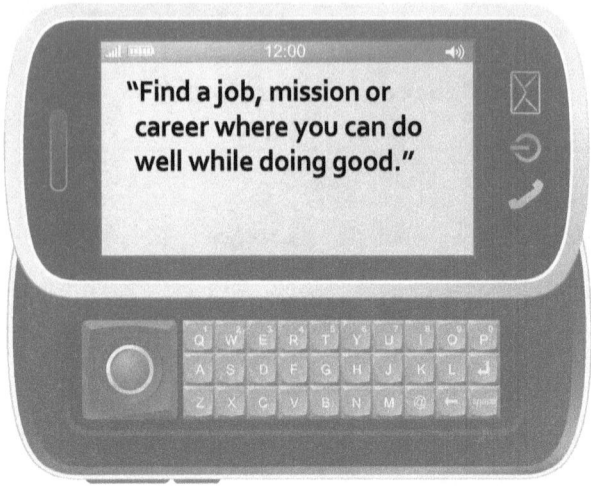

Dr. Dave Metcalf
Researcher,
University of Central Florida

 Your mission or job is supposed to enrich you, but it can also enrich others at the same time.

TEXTS 2 TEENS

Chapter 9: Work

Dr. Amy Henninger
US Defense Scientist

 "Has-beens" are proud of the impact they have had on the world. Nothing lasts forever except having done nothing at all.

TEXTS 2 TEENS

Sending the advice and wisdom that they desperately need

John Blair
Aviation Dispatcher, Boeing

 It takes coal millions of years to become a diamond—but only if they stick to it until they are finished.

TEXTS 2 TEENS

Chapter 9: Work

 We all make mistakes. Be smart enough to stop making them when you see that something is going wrong.

TEXTS 2 TEENS

Sending the advice and wisdom that they desperately need

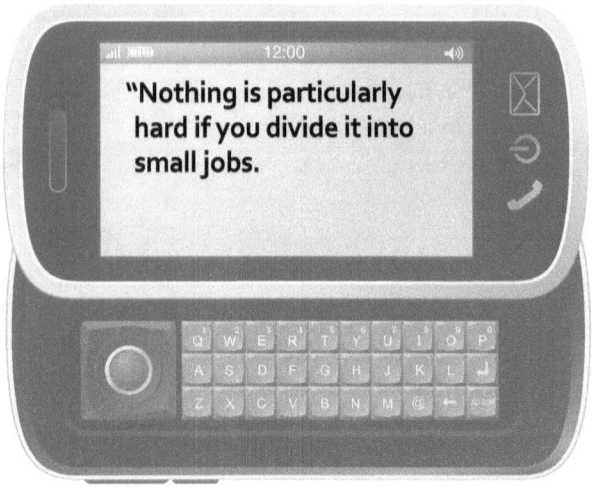

"Nothing is particularly hard if you divide it into small jobs."

John Blair
Aviation Dispatcher, Boeing

Big accomplishments are made one day at a time. People who do big things really do many little things that all add up. No one can build a bridge in a single day.

TEXTS 2 TEENS

Chapter 9: Work

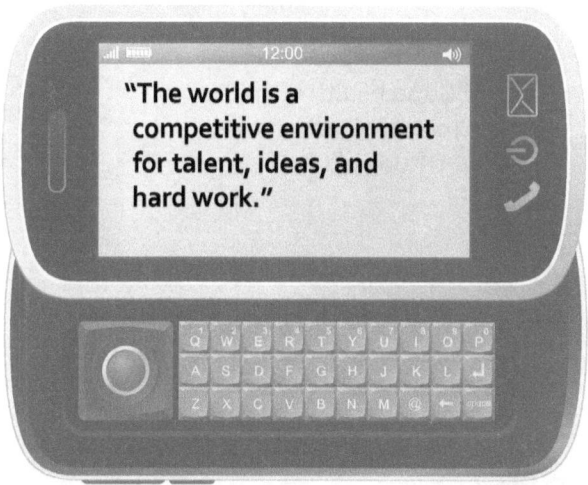

There are many people who are after the same things that you want. You have to show the world that you want them more by working for them.

TEXTS 2 TEENS

Sending the advice and wisdom that they desperately need

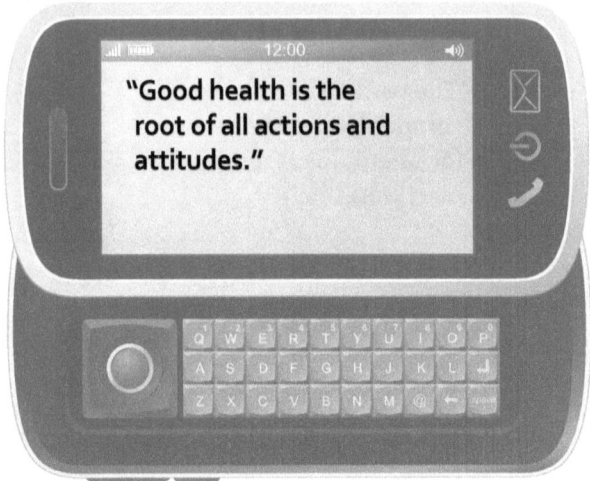

 Your physical health has a direct link to your thoughts and actions. A healthy body creates a healthy mind and an active life.

Chapter 9: Work

Tracy McSheery
VP, Phase Space

Too many people expect to be handed a career when they graduate from college simply because they finished. Every great person you admire had to work, practice, fail and get up and try again. Don't expect any other path to success. Learn to fail and forgive yourself. Those who avoid failure lose any chance at true success.

TEXTS 2 TEENS

Sending the advice and wisdom that they desperately need

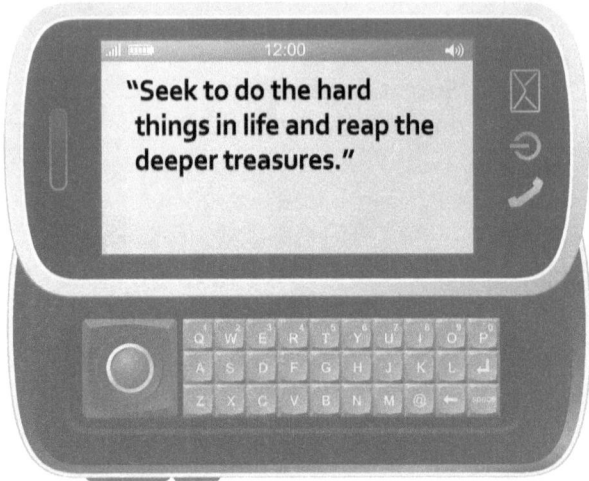

Ron Sprinkle
Senior Architect, SAIC

The treasures of accomplishing hard things are greater than the sum of many easy things. Challenge yourself to go further.

TEXTS 2 TEENS

Chapter 9: Work

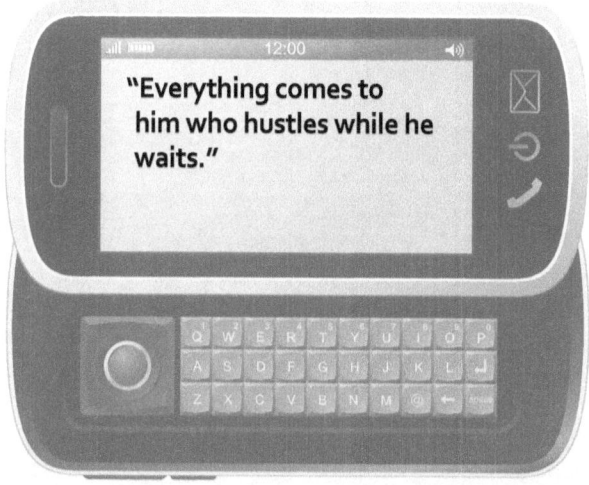

Thomas Edison
Inventor

 Edison did not create his inventions by sitting idlely waiting for inspiration.

www.ingramcontent.com/pod-product-compliance
Lightning Source LLC
Chambersburg PA
CBHW031250290426
44109CB00012B/509